The
Pennsylvania Colony

by Dennis B. Fradin

Consultant: Cynthia J. Little, Ph.D.
The Historical Society of Pennsylvania
Philadelphia, Pennsylvania

 CHILDRENS PRESS ®
CHICAGO

Library of Congress Cataloging-in-Publication Data

Fradin, Dennis B.
    The Pennsylvania colony / by Dennis B. Fradin.
       p. cm.
    Includes index.
    Summary: A history of the colony of Pennsylvania, from the time of the
earliest European settlers to the aftermath of the battle for independence that
resulted in statehood. Includes biographical sketches of some individuals
prominent in Pennsylvania history.
    ISBN 0-516-00390-9
    1. Pennsylvania—History—Colonial period, ca. 1600-1775—Juvenile
literature. 2. Pennsylvania—History—Revolution, 1775-1783—Juvenile
literature. [1. Pennsylvania—History—Colonial period, ca. 1600-1775.
2. Pennsylvania—History—Revolution, 1775-1783.] I. Title.
F152.F75   1988
974.8'02—dc19
                                          88-11975
                                            CIP
                                            AC

Childrens Press®, Chicago
Copyright © 1988 by Regensteiner Publishing Enterprises, Inc.
All rights reserved. Published simultaneously in Canada.
Printed in the United States of America.

    8 9 10 R 97 96

Table of Contents

The *Shield*, passing the future site of Philadelphia

Chapter I

Introduction to the Keystone State

The province of Pennsylvania is a healthy one; for the most part it has good soil, good air and water, lots of high mountains, and lots of flat land. There are many woods, and where these are not inhabited, there is natural forest through which flow many small and large rivers. The land is also very fertile, and all kinds of grain flourish.

Gottlieb Mittelberger, describing Pennsylvania in 1756

Seal of Penn's Colony

During the 1600s, people in England were denied religious freedom. From time to time, people who did not belong to the Church of England were stripped of their property and/or jailed. Many of the first English people who colonized America in the 1600s came so they could worship freely. The Pilgrims who colonized Massachusetts in 1620 sought such a haven. Later in the century, Pennsylvania was also colonized by people seeking a place where they could worship as they pleased.

An advertisement for
settlement in
Pennsylvania published
in 1681

In 1680, Englishman William Penn made an offer to England's King Charles II. The king owed Penn about 16,000 pounds, which was worth about $80,000 then.

Penn asked that, instead of paying back the money, the king grant him land in America.

For three reasons, the king agreed. First, William Penn belonged to the Religious Society of Friends, popularly known as the *Quakers*. If Penn founded a colony in America, England would probably be rid of many Quakers. Second, the English had claimed a piece of land south of New York in 1664 without colonizing it. If Penn and his followers colonized this land, England would have a stronger hold on it. Third, since the English considered America not very valuable, Charles probably thought he was paying off his debt rather cheaply.

In 1681, the king granted William Penn a large tract of land south of New York. Penn wanted to call his colony *New Wales* because the stories he heard about its mountainous land reminded him of Wales, just west of England. But King Charles had an assistant from Wales who objected to this name being given to such an unsettled place. Since his land was wooded, Penn then suggested

Sylvania, a Latin word meaning *forest*. The king wanted to honor the Penn family name, however, because William's father had been his good friend. Joining *Penn* with *Sylvania*, the king coined the name *Pennsylvania*.

Pennsylvania proved to be one of the most successful of England's thirteen American colonies. Thousands of people from England and several other European countries went there and set up farms. By 1710, the colony's biggest city, Philadelphia, was the largest city in the American colonies. By 1770, only Virginia had more people than Pennsylvania.

The Harris Frontier House in Harrisburg, Pennsylvania

During the 1770s, Pennsylvania played a leading role in the colonies' fight for independence from Great Britain. The convention of colonial delegates known as the First Continental Congress met in Philadelphia in 1774 to discuss their troubles with Britain. On July 4, 1776, the Second Continental Congress, also meeting in Philadelphia, adopted the Declaration of Independence, which explained why Americans wanted their country to stand on its own.

During the Revolutionary War, which America waged to free itself from Britain, several major battles were fought near Philadelphia. And before going on to win the war, George Washington and his cold, sick, and hungry troops spent an awful winter at Valley Forge, Pennsylvania, about twenty-five miles west of Philadelphia.

Coat of Arms of Pennsylvania

In the year 1800, Washington, D.C., became the capital of the United States, but most of the time between 1776 and 1800 the nation's capital was located in Pennsylvania. The town of Lancaster, Pennsylvania, served as the capital for one day in 1777. York, Pennsylvania, served as the capital for nine months in 1777–1778. Philadelphia was the country's capital four different times with the longest stint lasting from 1790 to 1800.

The United States Constitution (which contains the country's laws) was created in Philadelphia in 1787. Delaware, which had once been part of Pennsylvania, became the first state when it approved the Constitution on December 7, 1787. Pennsylvania became the second state by approving the Constitution five days later on December 12.

In the two centuries since it became a state, Pennsylvania has contributed a great deal to the nation. Pennsylvanians strongly opposed slavery before and during the Civil War (1861–1865) and

Gettysburg National Military Park, site of the greatest battle ever fought in North or South America (left) and Independence Hall, Philadelphia (right)

helped many slaves escape to Canada along the series of hiding places known as the "underground railroad." The bloodiest battle of the Civil War—and the greatest battle ever fought in North or South America—took place at the little town of Gettysburg, Pennsylvania, in summer of 1863. The North's victory at Gettysburg was a key cause of the South's defeat in the Civil War. Several months later, President Abraham Lincoln gave his famous Gettysburg Address at the battlefield.

During the 1800s and on into this century, Pennsylvania has been a leading farming and mining state. Today Pennsylvania is a leader in

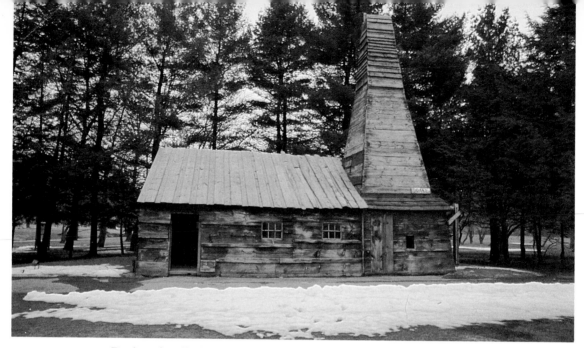

Drake oil well, the nation's first commercial oil well

producing such farm goods as milk, mushrooms, eggs, and apples. It is one of the top states for mining coal and stone. In 1859, the nation's first successful oil well was drilled in Pennsylvania, and today the state is still a large oil producer.

Pennsylvania is also a manufacturing center. Pittsburgh, the state's second largest city after Philadelphia, is called the *Steel City* because of all the steel and pig iron made there. Pennsylvania is the country's third leading steel-making state behind Indiana and Ohio. Other products made in Philadelphia, Pittsburgh, Erie, Allentown, Scranton, and Pennsylvania's other cities include food products like chocolate, machinery, tools, clothing, paper, and glass.

Harrisburg, located in south-central Pennsylvania, is the capital of Pennsylvania. The state has two well-known nicknames. Due to its geography, Pennsylvania is called the *Keystone State*. The keystone in the center of an arch holds the other stones in place. Similarly, Pennsylvania was the center of the arch formed by the English colonies. Because William Penn and other Quakers founded the Pennsylvania Colony, Pennsylvania is also called the *Quaker State*.

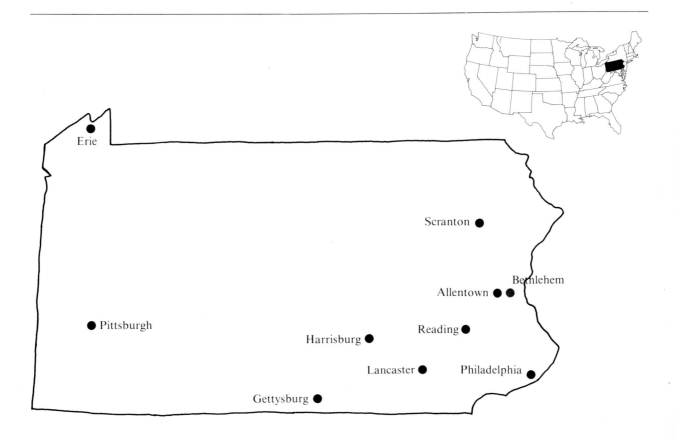

Astronaut Charles
Conrad, Jr.

Some very famous people have made their homes in the Keystone State. The frontiersman Daniel Boone was born in Pennsylvania as was the fifteenth president of the United States, James Buchanan, who was born in a log cabin near Mercersburg. Benjamin Franklin was born in Boston, but lived much of his life in Philadelphia. Pennsylvania has produced other famous people, such as the flag-maker Betsy Ross, the artist Mary Cassatt, and the astronaut Charles Conrad, Jr., commander of the second manned-lunar landing.

Philadelphia Library, founded by Benjamin Franklin in 1731

The Liberty Bell

Pennsylvania is also a leading state for tourism. Each year, thousands of people visit Pennsylvania to enjoy its lovely mountains and waterfalls, and its pretty little towns, some of which date back to colonial days. Other tourists come to see the state's historic attractions, including Revolutionary and Civil War sites, Philadelphia's famed Liberty Bell, and the city's Independence Hall, where the Declaration of Independence and the United States Constitution were both adopted.

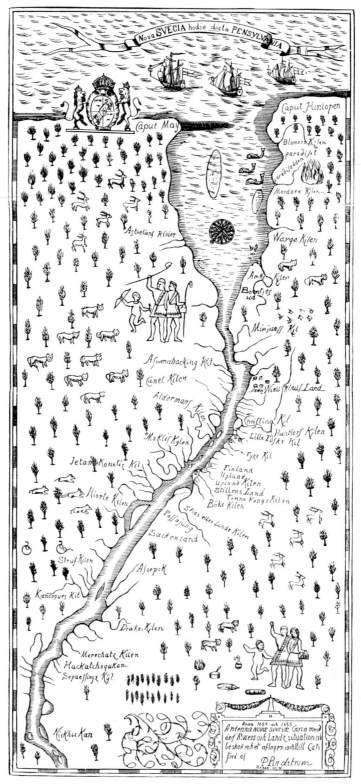

Lower Delaware in 1650

Chapter II

The Indians of Pennsylvania

*The one who knows how to associate rightly with
the [Indians will learn that they] are a trustworthy
and good-hearted folk, when they are not angered,
and even brave-hearted [enough] to risk death for
their good friends.*

> Swedish colonist Peter Lindeström, who
> came to Pennsylvania in the 1650s

People first came to Pennsylvania at least
10,000 years ago. The early Pennsylvanians did
not live in one place, but moved about while
chasing animal herds across the countryside. The
animals provided meat and clothing for these
early people, who may have been the ancestors of
Pennsylvania's Indian tribes of later centuries.

By the early 1600s, there were about 15,000
Indians living in Pennsylvania. They belonged to
several tribes, inculding the Delaware, the Susquehannock, the Erie, and a group sometimes called
the Monongahela People.

The Delaware were an important tribe. They
lived along and not far from the Delaware River in
what is now eastern Pennsylvania, northern

Delaware, the New York City region of New York State, and New Jersey. The Delaware called themselves the *Lenni Lenape*, meaning "Original People" or "Genuine People." Colonists from England later gave the name of the English Lord De La Warr to Delaware Bay and River, the Delaware Colony (later the state of Delaware), and also to the Indians who called themselves the *Lenni Lenape*. The English name *Delaware*, rather than *Lenni Lenape*, is usually used to identify this tribe.

Delaware villages varied in size from between several dozen to a few hundred people. They built two kinds of dwellings—*longhouses* and *wigwams*. Made of wood and covered with bark, a longhouse was home to several related families that each had its own section of the building. Wigwams were made of the same basic materials as longhouses but were dome-shaped huts.

Both mothers and fathers provided food for their families. The women grew the crops. Using hoes made of wood or shells, they broke up the soil and then planted corn in little dirt mounds. Between the corn mounds, beans and squash were planted. The women also gathered berries and roots to feed their families.

Delaware Indian family in 1653

The men did the hunting and fishing. In those days deer, bears, and many kinds of game birds were abundant. The men hunted with bows and arrows and fished with nets and bone hooks.

The animals and crops provided the Delaware with many everyday items besides food. Animal skins were made into clothes and blankets. Small animal bones were made into needles and fishing hooks. Turkey feathers, porcupine quills, and colorful corn kernels were used as decorations. Cornhusks were woven into mats and baskets, and made into children's dolls.

When they learned to walk, children began helping with the family's work. Little boys and girls stood watch in the fields to scare birds away from the growing crops. Older girls helped their mothers plant and harvest the crops and cook the stews, soups, and succotash (beans and corn cooked together). Older boys helped their fathers make dugout canoes and bows and arrows, and also hunted and fished with them. The Delaware had no schools. Young people learned how to do things by working alongside their elders.

Like most Indians, the Delaware were very religious. They believed in many nature gods that were ruled over by a supreme god, often known as the Great Spirit, or the Creator. The Delaware *shamans* (priests) taught that there were twelve heavens. Eleven of them were inhabited by important gods—the Sun, the Moon, the Earth, the Corn Mother, Water, Fire, the Home, and the gods of the North, South, East, and West. The twelfth and highest heaven was the Great Spirit's dwelling place.

The Delaware built their homes facing east, so that at every dawn they could pray to the rising

MANETTO INDIANORUM,

"Maniton" carving over Delaware Indian door

Sun. Each spring the Delaware held their Corn Dance ceremony to honor the Corn Mother, who protected the growing crops. They also held a Harvest Festival and other ceremonies during the year to honor their gods. In some cases these religious festivals lasted twelve days because twelve was the Delawares' sacred number. The Indians smoked tobacco while praying in the belief that the smoke carried their prayers up to the gods.

The Delaware thought that men were better at making decisions than women, but that women were better judges of character. Men served as the *sachems*, or chiefs, of the tribe. The sachems settled arguments and had important roles in religious ceremonies. The elderly women chose the sachems and dismissed ones who were not doing their job well.

Other tribes considered the Delaware to be a generous and honorable people. They were also a peaceful people who settled arguments between other tribes. As a result, the Delaware earned the complimentary nickname "the Grandfathers."

Much is known about the Delaware because they were the main tribe that the early colonists encountered in the Pennsylvania region. The several thousand Delaware who now live mainly in Oklahoma, Wisconsin, and Canada are also a source of information about the tribe.

The three other major tribes in Pennsylvania in the early 1600s were the Susquehannock, the Erie, and the Monongahela People. The Susquehannock (also known as the Conestoga) lived along the Susquehanna River about a hundred miles to the west of the Delaware Indians and also lived along the same river in what is now New York and Maryland. The Erie made their homes along Lake Erie in northwestern Pennsylvania and northeastern Ohio. The Monongahela People lived in southwestern Pennsylvania along the Monongahela River.

Like the Delaware, these three tribes hunted, fished, raised crops, and worshiped many gods. But few details are known about their ways of life. The Susquehannocks were wiped out by the colonists and by disease over two centuries ago. The Erie were destroyed in battles with the Iroquois Indians during the 1600s. The Monongahela People disappeared over two centuries ago, although some think they were the ancestors of the Shawnee tribe of a slightly later period.

Although about 11,000 Indians live in Pennsylvania today, relatively few of them belong to tribes that lived in the region before the colonists arrived. However, some place names serve as reminders of those early Indian tribes. The Susquehannock's name is preserved in the Susquehanna River, Susquehanna County, and the town of Susquehanna Depot, Pennsylvania. Lake Erie and the city of Erie in northwestern Pennsylvania are named for the Erie Indians. And the Delaware share their name with not only a state, river, and bay, but also Delaware County in southeastern Pennsylvania.

The Swedes called their North American Colony New Sweden.

Chapter III

Exploration and First Colonists

The winter immediately set in, bitterly cold; the river and the creeks froze up, and nobody was able to get near us [to help]. The sharpness of the winter lasted far into the month of March; so that, if [not for] some rye and corn . . . I myself and all the people with me on the island would have starved to death. . . .

Governor Johan Printz, describing the winter of 1645–1646 when Pennsylvania was part of New Sweden

FIRST EXPLORATION

The English and the French began colonizing North America at about the same time, but were interested in different regions. The English were most interested in what is now the United States, while the French focused most of their efforts on Canada. The first permanent English colony in America was built at Jamestown, Virginia, in 1607. The next year the French explorer Samuel de Champlain founded the village of Quebec, Canada, which is now that country's oldest city.

Although only sixteen years old at the time, an adventurous Frenchman named Étienne Brulé (1592?–1633?) helped Champlain found Quebec. A few years later, in 1615–1616, Champlain sent Brulé on an exploring trip down the Susquehanna River.

Brulé and his Indian guides started out at the Susquehanna's head waters in what is now New York State. They paddled their canoe south into what is now Pennsylvania, traveled through Pennsylvania, and possibly went all the way south to where the Susquehanna empties into Chesapeake Bay in Maryland. Brulé's canoe trip through Pennsylvania is thought to have been the first exploration of the region by a European.

The French were not interested in colonizing Pennsylvania, though. They were more interested in trading with the Indians for furs than in building colonies. They also did not want to anger the British, who had a growing interest in colonizing what is now the East Coast of the United States.

SWEDISH RULE

Two other countries wanted to colonize what is now the northeastern United States. One was Sweden, the other The Netherlands.

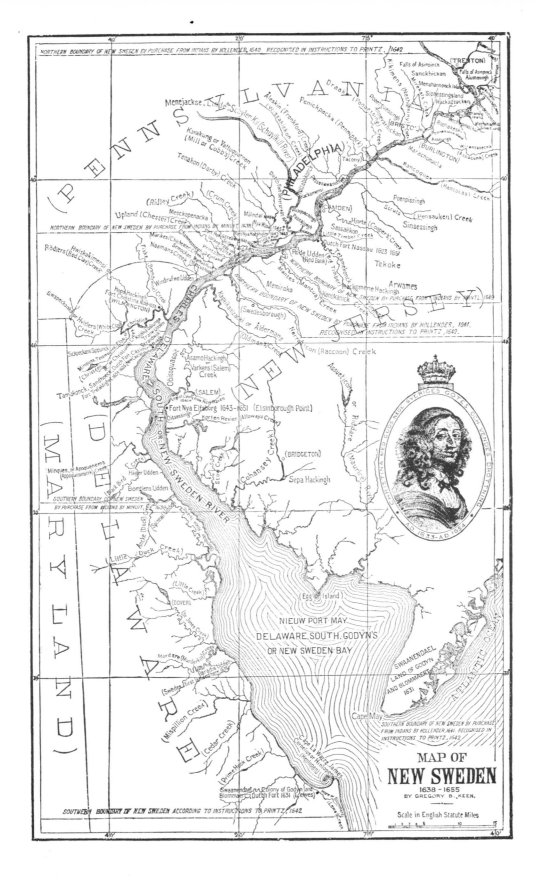

MAP OF
NEW SWEDEN
1638 - 1655
BY GREGORY B. KEEN.

Scale in English Statute Miles

Johan Printz

Under King Gustavus Adolphus (1594-1632), Sweden had begun to gain European territory in the early 1600s. After the king's death, his daughter, Queen Christina (1626-1689) and her chancellor, Axel Oxenstierna, made plans to colonize America. Two ships, the *Key of Kalmar* (named after a city in Sweden) and the *Flying Griffin*, sailed out of Sweden in late 1637. The two ships arrived at Delaware Bay in spring of 1638. The Swedes then began building a colony along the Delaware River in what are now parts of Delaware, Pennsylvania, and New Jersey. They called their colony *New Sweden.*

At first New Sweden's capital was Fort Christina at what is now Wilmington, Delaware, but the Swedes soon realized that they had to find a safer location for their capital. In early 1643, Johan Printz, the new governor of New Sweden, arrived. Printz relocated the capital of New Sweden farther up the Delaware River, at Tinicum Island, not far from what is now Philadelphia. Governor Printz, who was called "Big Belly" by the Indians because he weighed about 400 pounds, directed the building of houses, a fort, a church, and a school at Tinicum Island. The Swedes called this settlement *New Gothenburg*, after the city of

The Swedes built the first log cabins in America.

Gothenburg (now called Göteborg), Sweden. New Gothenburg was the first permanent European town in what is now Pennsylvania.

Many New Sweden colonists built log cabins and set up farms. In fact, within what is now Delaware, they built the first log cabins in America. New Sweden never grew very large in population, however, and at its peak was home to only several hundred people.

DUTCH RULE

The Dutch (people of The Netherlands) were interested in the Pennsylvania region, too. In 1609, Henry Hudson explored Delaware Bay for the Dutch. Hudson turned back toward the ocean before reaching the Delaware River, however, and so he never reached Pennsylvania. In 1615, the Dutch explorer Cornelius Hendricksen did reach Pennsylvania when he sailed up the Delaware River to the site of Philadelphia.

During the 1620s, the Dutch founded what they called their *New Netherland* colony in America. Its heart was what is now New York State, but it also covered part of New Jersey, Delaware, and Connecticut. The Dutch claimed that some of the towns of New Sweden stood on land that belonged to them. In 1655, the governor of New Netherland, Peter Stuyvesant, led hundreds of soldiers into New Sweden, capturing it without a fight. New Sweden, including Pennsylvania, then became part of New Netherland.

The changeover from Swedish to Dutch rule in 1655 was peaceful. The Swedish flag came down, and the Dutch colors went up. The settlers who wanted to remain were allowed to do so, and their way of life changed very little. There were only a

Fur trapper sets animal traps.

few dozen settlers living in Pennsylvania anyway, many of them farmers and fur traders.

Sweden's rule over Pennsylvania had lasted a little over ten years, between 1643 and 1655. Like the Swedes, the Dutch did not provide the resources and people that were required for successful colonization of America. Dutch rule over Pennsylvania lasted just nine years, between 1655 and 1664. While under Dutch control, Pennsylvania experienced little growth. Southeastern

Pennsylvania in the region of the Delaware River remained the only part of the territory that was colonized. By the early 1660s there were only several hundred non-Indians in Pennsylvania, most of them Swedes, Finns, and Dutch.

ENGLAND TAKES OVER

After a number of explorations, England claimed what is now the East Coast of the United States. By the 1660s, England controlled most of the East Coast between Maine and South Carolina with the exception of New Netherland.

Charles II became king of England in 1660. Four years later he gave his brother, James, the land the Dutch had named New Netherland. The king instructed his brother to use force if the Dutch fought to keep the territory.

James organized a large fleet of warships and sent them to New Amsterdam (now New York City), the capital of New Netherland. When they saw the ships' guns aimed at their city, the people of New Amsterdam begged Governor Peter Stuyvesant to surrender. Although he wanted to fight, "Stubborn Pete" saw that it was useless. In early September of 1664, he surrendered all of New

Governor Peter Stuyvesant surrenders New Amsterdam to the English.

Netherland. Now New York, New Jersey, Delaware, Connecticut, and Pennsylvania passed into English hands. They were to remain under English control for over a century.

During the next few years some English people came to Pennsylvania. But the colony was still largely unsettled when in 1681 King Charles II granted the area to a man named William Penn.

Quaker
preaching in
Pennsylvania.

Chapter IV

William Penn's "Holy Experiment"

This day my country was confirmed to me . . . by the name of Pennsylvania, a name the king would give it in honor of my father. . . . My God that has given it to me . . . will, I believe, bless and make it the seed of a nation.

> *William Penn, writing on the spring day in 1681 when he was granted Pennsylvania*

George Fox

In about 1647, an Englishman named George Fox (1624–1691) founded a religious group called the Religious Society of Friends. Fox taught that since all people were equal to God, everyone should be treated with love and respect. He said that war was wrong and that Friends should not serve in armies. The Friends, who believed that spiritual values were more important than possessions, dressed and lived simply. Believing that each person contained a bit of God, Fox and his followers considered ministers unnecessary. The Friends worshiped silently in their meeting-houses, although anyone who felt inspired could stand and speak to the congregation.

The Friends had many enemies in England, where most of the people belonged to the Church of England. In a country that was almost always at war, the Friends' stance on warfare was very unpopular. And in an age when important people expected special treatment, the Friends annoyed the rich and famous by treating them the same as the poor and unknown. For example, the Friends would not take off their hats for anyone—not even the king and queen.

Once when Fox was in court, he told a judge "to tremble at the word of the Lord." Because of Fox's reference to trembling, the judge called him a "Quaker," and soon all the members of Fox's sect were being called Quakers. England persecuted the Quakers, who by 1682 numbered 60,000. Between 1661 and the early 1680s, about 15,000 of them were imprisoned, and at least 450 of them died due to various kinds of mistreatment.

A young man named William Penn, who was jailed several times for his beliefs, was one of the best-known Quakers. By 1680, Penn had decided that the Quakers needed a new home where they could pursue their beliefs in peace. He asked Charles II to repay a debt by granting him land in America. After some haggling with his brother James, to whom he had previously given the

Coat of Arms of the Penn family

William Penn at age 28

territory, Charles agreed to the deal in 1681. The king named the colony *Pennsylvania* for the Penn family.

Pennsylvania was a carefully planned colony. Penn wrote to a friend that his colony would be a "holy experiment," meaning that he was going to give people the chance to live in love and harmony according to Quaker beliefs. With that in mind, Penn decided that his colony should be a haven for non-Quakers, too. He distributed pamphlets about Pennsylvania to Quakers and non-Quakers in England, Ireland, Wales, Scotland, Germany, The Netherlands, and Switzerland. Hundreds of people responded and purchased land from Penn.*

William Penn could not go to his colony until 1682. But in spring of 1681, he sent his cousin William Markham to Pennsylvania as his deputy governor. Markham brought a letter from Penn to the Swedes, Finns, Dutch, and English who had lived in Pennsylvania before it became Penn's colony. Calling them "My Friends," Penn assured the old colonists that "you shall be governed by laws of your own making, and live a free . . . people."

In fall of 1681, Penn sent a letter to the Indians which began:

> *My Friends:—There is one great God and power that hath made the world and all things therein, to whom you, and I, and all people owe their being and well-being, and to whom you and I must one day give an account for all that we have done in the world.*

Penn also said that he wanted the Indians and the colonists to "always live together as neighbors and friends." He explained that he had a "great love and regard" for the Indians and hoped to win their "love and friendship." He finished by saying

* For more information about the Pennsylvania Charter see page 149

36

that any colonists who harmed the Indians would be punished and that he looked forward to meeting the Native Americans. He signed the letter, "your loving friend, William Penn."

This letter is one of the most remarkable documents of colonial times. Although the Indians had taught them to plant corn and survive in the new land, most colonists hated, disliked, or barely tolerated the Native Americans. These colonists were prejudiced. Like the men and women in England who persecuted people of different faiths, they would not admit that the Indians were as good as themselves.

William Penn, however, insisted that the Indians and the colonists were equals, despite differences in life-style. Ninety-five years before Thomas Jefferson wrote that "all men are created equal" in the Declaration of Independence, William Penn took steps towards putting that noble thought into action in Pennsylvania.

A few of Penn's colonists came to Pennsylvania in 1681, but large-scale settlement didn't start until the next year. In August of 1682, Penn and about a hundred others, mostly English Quakers, set sail for Pennsylvania aboard the *Welcome*. The colonists brought axes to cut down trees, cows

The *Welcome* carried about a hundred passengers.

and chickens to stock their farms, and even silverware and beds from home. During the more than 3,000-mile journey between England and America, smallpox broke out aboard the *Welcome*, killing about 30 people. Penn, who was immune to smallpox because he had suffered from the disease as a child, helped nurse the sick.

After a two-month voyage, the *Welcome* reached New Castle, Delaware. Penn had been given title to the little colony of Delaware by James, the king's brother. Because Delaware was south of Pennsylvania and was divided into three counties, it became known as Pennsylvania's *Three Lower Counties*.

Penn and his followers spent a day at New Castle, Delaware, and then the *Welcome* sailed twenty miles up the river to a little town that the Dutch settlers had called *Oplandt*. This was the spot where Penn first stepped onto Pennsylvania soil. Reportedly he asked a Friend: "What would thou call this place?" The man answered "Chester," because Chester, England, had been his hometown. Located fifteen miles southwest of Philadelphia, Chester was Pennsylvania's first capital between 1681 and 1683.

James I

From Chester, a barge took Penn a little farther up the Delaware to a place the Indians called *Coaquannock*, meaning "Grove of Pines." There work was already underway on the new capital that William Penn had planned out while still in England. Penn named this town *Philadelphia*, meaning *Brotherly Love* in Greek. Penn's dream was that Philadelphia would be an almost heavenly place where everyone would live in peace and understanding.

Penn wanted Philadelphia to be not only spiritually good, but physically beautiful. Many colonial towns were dirty, crowded, disease-ridden firetraps. Penn planned Philadelphia as a "green country town" that would have broad streets and houses on large lots. When he arrived, Philadelphia had only about ten houses. But soon the newcomers were putting up more houses and laying out streets in a grid pattern. Several of the Philadelphia streets that are important today were named by Penn. Among them are Chestnut, Walnut, Spruce, and Pine streets.

William Penn planned and named the streets of Philadelphia

Within a year Philadelphia was home to about eighty families; by 1685 about 2,500 colonists lived there.* The city grew so quickly that some colonists lived in caves along the banks of the Delaware River while their homes were being built. Thanks to Penn's careful planning, Philadelphia was the largest city in the colonies by 1710. It was also the loveliest according to many people.

Penn had created a constitution for Pennsylvania while still in England. Called the *First Frame of Government*, it detailed Pennsylvania's government. William Penn was to be governor. The colony was also to have a two-house legislature—an upper body called the *Council* and a lower house called the *Assembly*.

The Council and Assembly were to be elected by Pennsylvania's *freemen*, or male citizens. The freemen comprised less than half the adult population. Women, indentured servants (people who worked for wealthy Pennsylvanians who had paid their passage to America), and slaves could not vote. The freemen were to elect the seventy-two-man Council, which would help the governor propose laws and also help him carry out the laws if they were passed. The freemen were also to elect the 200-man Assembly which would discuss and

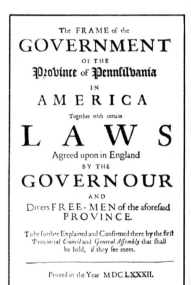

The FRAME of the
GOVERNMENT
OF THE
Province of Pennsilvania
IN
AMERICA
Together with certain
L A W S
Agreed upon in England
BY THE
GOVERNOUR
AND
Divers FREE-MEN of the aforesaid
PROVINCE.
To be further Explained and Confirmed there by the first Provincial Council and General Assembly that shall be held, if they see meet.

Printed in the Year MDCLXXXII.

The Frame of
Government, 1682

* For more information about land ownership see pages 150 and 151

41

then vote on the laws proposed by the governor and his Council.

The legislature first met at Chester, the colony's first capital, in late 1682. At about that time, William Penn decided to meet with the Indians in person to assure them of his friendship and love. This meeting between Penn and the Indians is thought to have been held a little north of what is now downtown Philadelphia. Penn brought several Pennsylvania lawmakers with him to the meeting, and representatives of at least three tribes—the Delaware, the Susquehannock, and the Shawnee—also attended.

The wampum belt given to William Penn by Delaware Chief Tamanend

"The Great Spirit who made me and you, who rules the heavens and the Earth, and who knows the innermost thoughts of men, knows that I and my friends have a hearty desire to live in peace and friendship with you," Penn told the Indians through an interpreter. The Indians and the colonists would always respect the rights of the Native Americans. In return, the Delaware Chief

42

Tamanend gave Penn a wampum (bead) belt with a picture of a Quaker and an Indian clasping hands on it. This friendship belt remained with the Penn family for 175 years. In 1857 Penn's descendant Granville John Penn gave it to the Historical Society of Pennsylvania in Philadelphia, where it can still be seen.

Long after William Penn left Pennsylvania, the Indians honored the Great Treaty that they had made with him in 1682. The Indians kept their word even after many of them were cheated out of their lands by Pennsylvanians in the 1700s.

The Great Treaty between William Penn and the Indians

The First Frame of Government was much less successful than the Great Treaty. Penn knew that the people would have ideas of their own, so he hadn't expected the First Frame to last forever. But he was surprised when Pennsylvanians wanted changes in their government almost immediately. Basically, they wanted more of a say in the government, which was the story throughout the thirteen colonies until America broke away from Britain completely during the Revolutionary War.

In spring of 1683, Penn offered his colony a new constitution, called the *Second Frame of Government*. The Second Frame granted some of the requests for more of a say in the government, but Penn refused requests to let the Assembly propose laws like the Council. Nevertheless, both houses accepted the Second Frame of Government and it became the law in April of 1683. That same year Pennsylvania's capital was moved from Chester to Philadelphia, which remained the capital until 1799.

Meanwhile, Penn was having an argument about the Pennsylvania-Maryland boundary with the proprietor of Maryland, Lord Baltimore, who wanted much of southern Pennsylvania. Finally Penn decided to return to England to present his case to the king. After directing the Council to govern the colony in his absence, Penn left in August of 1684. He couldn't know it at the time, but Penn was to return to Pennsylvania for just one more short stay, fifteen years later.

William Penn meeting with the colonists.

WILLIAM PENN (1644-1718)

William Penn

Born in London, William Penn was the son of Sir William Penn, a navy officer and later an admiral. William's mother was very religious, and it was probably from her that he developed his deep interest in religion.

When William was twelve years old, he had two religious experiences that made a deep impression on him. One day when he was alone in his room, he suddenly felt God's presence. After that, he always felt that God was nearby. The second event occurred when the Penn family visited some property they owned in Ireland. William heard the Quaker leader Thomas Loe speak and was very impressed by what he said.

Admiral Penn sent William to Oxford University in the hope that he would become a statesman. But William got in trouble at Oxford for refusing to attend Church of England services. Instead he held prayer meetings with some of his friends. For this he was fined and expelled from the university.

Admiral Penn, upset with William's behavior, whipped and beat his son while Mrs. Penn pleaded for leniency. Hoping to stop his son from being "different," Admiral Penn sent William on a European vacation, during which he mingled with many wealthy young people. The plan worked temporarily, for when William returned to England he seemed more interested in how he dressed than in religion.

But when William was in his early twenties, his father sent him to Ireland to manage the family estates. Again William met Thomas Loe. This time he was so impressed by Loe that he became a Quaker himself.

William Penn preached and wrote about the Quaker faith and about how all people had the right to worship as they pleased. When he was twenty-four he published a book called *The Sandy Foundation Shaken* in which he stated his beliefs. For publishing this "wicked" book, Penn was imprisoned in the Tower of London and was warned that he would "die a prisoner" unless he publicly gave up his Quaker beliefs. To this Penn answered, "My prison shall be my grave before I will budge a jot, for I owe my conscience to no mortal man."

During his imprisonment, Penn wrote another book, *No Cross, No Crown*, which explained Quaker beliefs. Admiral Penn begged his friend, James, the Duke of York, to arrange for William's release. James went to his brother, King Charles II, who ordered William freed. After spending nearly nine months in the Tower of London, William Penn was freed without having to "budge a jot" from his religious beliefs.

In 1670, William was arrested for preaching about the Quaker faith in the London streets. His trial was a landmark in the history of English law.

Although the judges wanted a "Guilty" verdict, the jury found Penn "Not guilty." Enraged, the judges ordered the jury to return to their chamber and make the proper verdict, but still they said "Not guilty." The jurors were fined and jailed, but they sued the judges and won. This established the rule that jurors must be free from threats by judges.

William Penn soon realized that there was "no hope in England" for religious freedom, and began dreaming of a haven where Quakers and everyone else could worship as they pleased. King Charles II had owed a large sum of money to Admiral Penn, and after the admiral died in 1670, he owed it to William. For payment of this debt, the young Quaker asked for and received a large tract of land, which became Pennsylvania.

Although William Penn visited his colony only twice for a period less than four years, he was loved by most of the colonists. Even more unusual, he was loved by the Indians. He always kept his word with the Indians and genuinely liked them.

Penn deserved to spend his last years peacefully in Pennsylvania. But after leaving Pennsylvania in 1701 to settle a problem with the king over the ownership of the colony, he never returned. William Penn suffered many misfortunes at the end of his life. Letters he received from Pennsylvania described its leaders' continual arguments. Penn was also cheated in business dealings. As a result, he spent a year in debtors' prison. His health was wrecked by this experience, and in 1712 he suffered a stroke that paralyzed him. The founder of Pennsylvania died six years later at the age of seventy-three.

William Penn's second wife, Hannah Penn, served as Pennsylvania's governor from the time of his stroke until her death in 1727. Their son John Penn then served as governor until 1746, and then another son, Thomas Penn, was governor until his death in 1775.

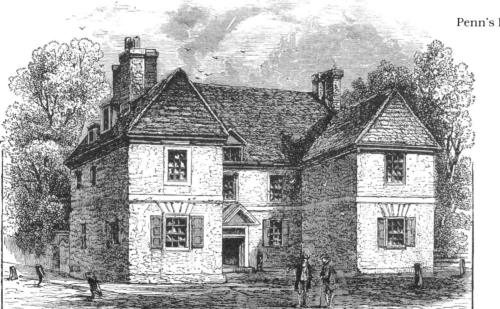

Penn's house

City of Philadelphia

Chapter V

The Growing Colony: 1684-1750

I have been with you, cared over you, and served you with [genuine] love; and you are beloved of me, and near to me, beyond utterance.

From a prayer William Penn wrote for Philadelphia in summer of 1684

A COLONIAL MELTING POT

The United States is sometimes called a "melting pot" because people of various ethnic and cultural backgrounds live in the country. In colonial times, New York and Pennsylvania were the two main melting pots. By the early 1700s, Pennsylvania was home to people of many religions and nationalities.

There were many Quakers in Pennsylvania, of course. There were also members of many other Protestant groups, including Lutherans, Reformed Germans, Church of Englanders, Presbyterians, Mennonites, Moravians, and the Amish. The Pennsylvania Colony was also home to some Catholics and Jewish people.

Pennsylvania Dutch Hex signs. Double-headed eagle (above) stands for Strength and Courage and the Welcome sign (below)

Thousands of the colonists had come from England, and thousands more had come from Germany, another country where there was widespread religious persecution. By the mid-1700s, about a third of Pennsylvania's population was of German origin. Despite the fact that they were not from The Netherlands, the Pennsylvania Germans became known as the *Pennsylvania Dutch*. The reason for this was that *Deutsch* means *German* in the German language. Their neighbors called the Pennsylvania Germans the *Pennsylvania Deutsch*, which was gradually changed to *Pennsylvania Dutch*. Thousands of descendants of the Pennsylvania Dutch colonists of the 1600s and 1700s still live in Pennsylvania.

MORE TOWNS AND PEOPLE

At first, the colonists lived almost completely in the Philadelphia region of southeastern Pennsylvania. However, some of the Philadelphia-area colonists, as well as some of the people who continually arrived from Europe, gradually moved farther out and built farms across the countryside. Lancaster, sixty-five miles west of Philadelphia, was founded in 1718. York, twenty-five miles west of Lancaster, was laid out in 1741.

The settlement of Reading, about fifty miles northwest of Philadelphia, came during the 1730s, while Bethlehem, fifty miles north of Philadelphia, was settled in the 1740s. However, central and western Pennsylvania for the most part were not settled until the late 1700s and afterwards.

As families grew and new settlers arrived, Pennsylvania's population increased rapidly. In 1680 only about 700 colonists lived in Pennsylvania. By 1700, the population had reached about 18,000, and by 1750 it had soared to 120,000.

The first American settlers

ARGUMENTS ABOUT GOVERNMENT

After William Penn's departure in 1684, there were many bitter disputes about the government in Pennsylvania. The Lower Counties (Delaware) were upset that they were not allowed representatives on the Council, the body that proposed laws for Pennsylvania and Delaware. The Assembly was angry that William Penn had not given it the power to propose laws.

To spite the Council, the Assembly turned down some of the Council's proposed laws. There were also a number of personal disputes among the lawmakers, some of whom hated each other. When William Penn was informed of the difficulties, he wrote back: "I am sorry at heart for your animosities. Cannot more friendly . . . courses be taken, to set matters right in an infant province? . . . For the love of God, me, and the poor country, be not so governmentish. . . ."

Penn coined the word "governmentish" to express his disappointment that Pennsylvanians were spending more time on political fights than on spiritual matters. He made a number of changes in the government, but the fights continued.

Events in England determined much of what happened in Pennsylvania during the late 1680s and the 1690s. In 1688, William Penn's friend King James II (who had succeeded his brother Charles) was overthrown. The new rulers, King William and Queen Mary, had Penn arrested several times because they thought he was still loyal to James.

Penn was charged with being an enemy to William and Mary. In 1692, they took Pennsylvania away from him and placed it under the rule of the governor of New York. However, in late 1693 Penn was acquitted of trying to help the deposed King James, and the next year Pennsylvania was restored to him. Penn was told to straighten out the problems with the Pennsylvania government.

William III of Orange

In 1696 William Markham, serving as Penn's acting governor in Pennsylvania, made governmental changes so that both houses could suggest laws. Then in 1699, William Penn was finally able to return to Pennsylvania for a two-year stay. Just before leaving Pennsylvania for the last time in late 1701, Penn wrote a new constitution that satisfied most of the people. Called the *Charter of Privileges*, it guaranteed certain rights and privileges of the freemen, and gave more control over the government to the people. The Charter also granted Delaware a separate legislature, although the governor of Pennsylvania still had jurisdiction over Delaware

Mary II

until the revolution. The Charter of Privileges was greatly respected and remained the law of Pennsylvania for seventy-five years, until 1776.

DISCRIMINATION IN PENNSYLVANIA

Colonial Pennsylvania granted more liberties to more people than did most of the other colonies. But colonial Pennsylvania did not grant the "liberty and justice for *all*" that Americans believe in today. Women, poor white people, black slaves, Jewish people, and the Indians were all victims of what we would call discrimination. Although they suffered less in Pennsylvania than they did in most other colonies, these five groups were excluded from power.

As in the other colonies, women could not vote. They also were excluded from running for public office, could not own property in their own name, and generally received less schooling than males. Most people at the time thought that women should be subject to the rule of their fathers, husbands, or older brothers. Most women's lives centered around maintaining a house and raising children.

Thousands of poor white Pennsylvanians were *indentured servants*—people who were almost

A New England Quaker
preaching in the streets

like slaves. These poor people had had their
voyage to Pennsylvania paid for by wealthy
colonists, but they had to work for these people—
often for about five years. Many indentured
families were split up when they reached Pennsylvania, as parents and children went to work for
different people. In many cases the family
members never saw each other again.

The indentured servants suffered under some
very cruel rules. If a man or woman died at sea
past the halfway point to America, the husband or

wife had to pay for the dead person's passage by working twice as long. If a man or woman arrived too sick to work, the husband or wife also had to work twice as many years. Children whose parents had died at sea had to work until the age of twenty-one to pay for the family's passage. Masters often mistreated their indentured servants. As a result, many indentured servants ran away.

As for slavery, many Pennsylvanians opposed it from the start and Pennsylvania was a leader in the antislavery movement. In 1688, the people of Germantown (now part of Philadelphia) passed the first antislavery resolution in the thirteen colonies. In 1775, Philadelphia Quakers created the first antislavery society, and in 1780 Pennsylvania became the first state to make widespread efforts to abolish slavery within its borders.

Nonetheless, William Penn and a number of other Quakers owned slaves, as did some other Pennsylvanians. By 1700, there were several hundred slaves in the colony, and by the mid-1700s there were several thousand. Although these numbers were much smaller than the slave populations of most other colonies, that was no consolation to the Pennsylvania slaves.

In nearly every place in Europe except The Netherlands, people of the Jewish faith were persecuted. Jews were welcome in Pennsylvania, and by the 1760s, a few dozen lived in the colony. However, according to the Charter of Privileges granted by William Penn in 1701, only people who "believe in Jesus Christ" could hold office. This meant that Jews were barred from holding office.

As in other colonies, many Pennsylvanians mistreated the Indians, especially after William Penn left. Some sold liquor to the Indians, and encouraged them to get drunk. Some lived on Indian lands without paying for them or asking permission. Even when they did purchase the Indians' lands, the colonists often cheated the Native Americans.

Delaware Chief Lapowinsa signed the "Walking Purchase" treaty.

The "Walking Purchase" of 1737 was a famous example of how the colonists found ways to trick the Indians in land deals. The Indians measured distances not by miles, but by such formulas as how far a person could walk in a certain time. In 1682, William Penn had purchased from the Delaware Indians a strip of land along the Delaware River in southeastern Pennsylvania. The tract was to extend as far north as a person could walk in three days. With several companions, William Penn walked off about forty miles in a day and a half. This was as much land as Penn thought the colonists needed at the time. However, it left another day and a half's walk that the colonists could make later when they wanted more land.

William Penn's son, Thomas, decided in 1737 that the Indians should give up the other day and a half's worth of land. In the spirit of the original deal, the Indians expected the colonists to walk off

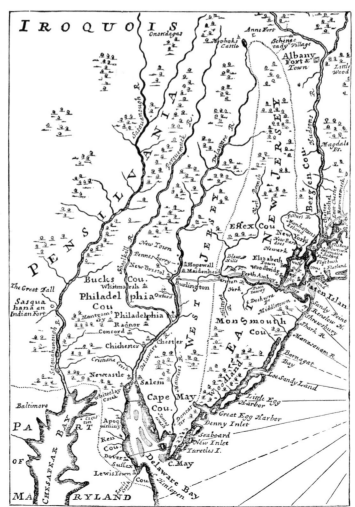

Map of the Province of Pennsylvania

Nedowaway of the Turtle tribe left Pennsylvania after being cheated of his land by the "Walking Purchase" treaty.

perhaps another forty miles. However, Thomas Penn hired three athletic men to make the walk and offered a large reward to the one who could travel the farthest. The prize was won by Edward Marshall, who in the thirty-six hours traveled over sixty-six miles, actually running much of the way.

The Delaware Indians lost a tremendous amount of land in southeastern Pennsylvania due to this "Walking Purchase." Many of them moved into northeastern Pennsylvania, but were soon driven out by the colonists from Connecticut, and had to flee into western Pennsylvania and Ohio. The Delaware never forgave the Pennsylvania colonists for tricking them out of their lands, and looked for the chance to strike back at them.

The plan of Philadelphia

Chapter VI

Life in Pennsylvania in 1750–1754

Pennsylvania . . . has become the general receptacle of foreigners from all countries and of all descriptions, many of whom soon take an active part in the politics of the state.

George Washington

LIFE IN PHILADELPHIA

In the year 1750, Philadelphia was Pennsylvania's largest city. Of the 120,000 colonists in Pennsylvania, about 15,000 of them lived in Philadelphia. Only Boston, Massachusetts, with 20,000 people, had a larger population than Philadelphia.

Because William Penn and his fellow Quakers founded it, Philadelphia was called the *Quaker City.* But by 1750, it was home to only eight hundred Quaker families, comprising about a fourth of the population. Philadelphia was also home to large numbers of German and Scotch-Irish people, and to people of many other nationalities.

Front of the Great Seal of the Province of Pennsylvania, 1712

Back of the Great Seal

Houses on High Street
in colonial Philadelphia

The clay along the river banks was good for making bricks, and by 1750 Philadelphia was known for its red brick buildings. Wealthy Philadelphians lived in brick mansions, but most people lived in small brick houses.

A great deal of street paving had taken place since the 1740s, but by 1750, many Philadelphians still complained about the remaining unpaved streets that had tree stumps and mud puddles. And because people piled up their garbage on them, many of Philadelphia's streets were filthy. In 1750, Mayor Thomas Lawrence ordered all families to keep the areas in front of their homes clean, but few people paid attention to the new law.

In 1751, the city installed whale-oil lamps on its main streets. At first, the new lamps were constantly smudged by smoke, but jack-of-all-trades Ben Franklin solved that problem by changing their design slightly. Then the main problem was young people breaking the lamps by hurling apples and rocks at them.

The Philadelphians of the early 1750s worked at a variety of jobs. Boston was the only colonial city that did more shipping than Philadelphia, and hundreds of Philadelphians worked at shipping-related jobs. Workers built sailing vessels in the city's shipyards. Merchants earned fortunes

Building a ship in the shipyard

buying and selling goods that went in and out of the city. Dock workers earned their living by unloading the ships that came up the Delaware River to Philadelphia, then loading them with new cargo.

A blacksmith making guns

Philadelphians also worked as blacksmiths (makers of horseshoes and other iron objects), tailors, carriage-makers, glass-makers, teachers, ministers, printers, booksellers, and lawyers. Hundreds worked in the city's more than one hundred taverns and inns.

Instead of working far from home as many people do today, the Philadelphians of the 1750s commonly had their shops and homes in the same building. Because many people could not read, some businesses had picture signs showing their names. For example, outside a metalworker's shop called the Golden Cup there was a picture of a golden cup. That way even people who could not read could find the shop.

The reason why so many people could not read was that Pennsylvania had no public-school system. There were a few church-run and private schools, and in the early 1750s several Phila-delphians set up free schools for the poor, but free public education did not get going until the mid-

Colonial school in
Pennsylvania

1800s. Until then, many people received little or
no schooling.

Wealthy families hired private tutors to teach
their young sons Latin, Greek, and other
advanced subjects. When they became teenagers,
some of the young men (but not the women)
atended college in Europe or in other colonies.
Pennsylvania's first college did not get its start
until 1751, when the Philadelphia Academy
opened. Ben Franklin was a founder of this school,
which today is the University of Pennsylvania.

Printing and publishing were very important in Philadelphia in the 1750s. The city had two main newspapers at the time—the *Pennsylvania Gazette* and the *Pennsylvania Journal.* Philadelphians sat in the city's taverns, inns, and parks passing the newspapers from person to person. Often someone would read the newspaper aloud so that people who didn't know how to read could learn about the news.

Ben Franklin's printing press

Like today, the front pages of the Philadelphia newspapers often related news from far away places like England, Italy, France, Russia, and Spain. But the stories weren't reported until several months had passed because it took that long to send the news by ship across the ocean. For example, the February 13, 1750, *Gazette* reported an event that had occurred in Moscow, Russia, on October 15 of the previous year! News stories from the other twelve colonies often took a few weeks before they were published in the Philadelphia papers.

The old newspapers reveal that the Philadelphians of the 1750s had many of the same interests as people today. There were many stories on local politics and events. The papers contained numerous advertisements from store owners who

First issue of the
Pennsylvania Gazette

wanted to sell their wares and from shipowners who wanted people to use their vessels. Lotteries were so popular that the winning numbers were sometimes printed in the paper. One aspect of the newspapers that makes them seem very old is the large number of rewards offered for the return of runaway slaves and indentured servants.

The most famous printer in Philadelphia at the time was Benjamin Franklin, publisher of the *Pennsylvania Gazette* and the extremely popular *Poor Richard's Almanack.* Each year a number of Philadelphia publishers came out with almanacs— booklets that told about the movements of heavenly bodies, gave weather forecasts, and offered little sayings. *Poor Richard's Almanack,*

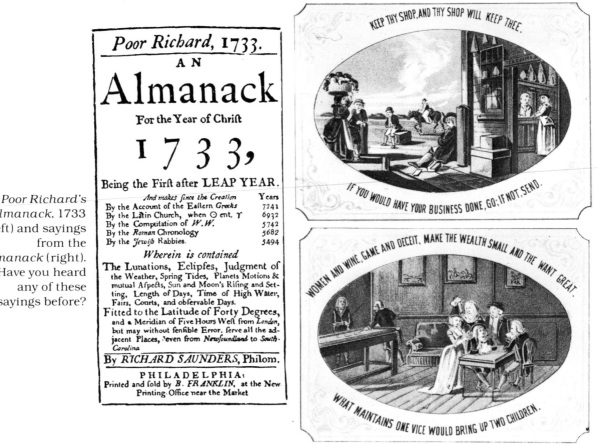

Poor Richard, 1733.
AN
Almanack
For the Year of Chrift
1733,
Being the Firft after LEAP YEAR.

And makes fince the Creation	Years
By the Account of the Eaftern *Greeks*	7241
By the Latin Church, when ☉ ent. ♈	6932
By the Computation of *W. W.*	5742
By the *Roman* Chronology	5682
By the *Jewifh* Rabbies.	5494

Wherein is contained
The Lunations, Eclipfes, Judgment of the Weather, Spring Tides, Planets Motions & mutual Afpects, Sun and Moon's Rifing and Setting, Length of Days, Time of High Water, Fairs, Courts, and obfervable Days.
Fitted to the Latitude of Forty Degrees, and a Meridian of Five Hours Weft from *London*, but may without fenfible Error, ferve all the adjacent Places, even from *Newfoundland* to *South Carolina.*
By *RICHARD SAUNDERS*, Philom.

PHILADELPHIA:
Printed and fold by *B. FRANKLIN*, at the New Printing-Office near the Market

Poor Richard's Almanack, 1733 (left) and sayings from the Almanack (right). Have you heard any of these sayings before?

published by Franklin from 1733 to 1758, was the second-most popular book in colonial America—behind only the Bible.

Franklin wrote his almanac under the name Richard Saunders, who was supposed to be "Poor Richard." The sayings in his almanac became household expressions around Philadelphia and later around the whole country. Parents who wanted their children to go to sleep would say, "As Poor Richard says, *Early to bed and early to rise, makes a man healthy, wealthy, and wise,*"

THE ART OF MAKING MONEY PLENTY

IN EVERY MAN'S POCKET; BY

Doctor Franklin

At this ⧫ the complaint is t [hat] [times] s, so s[in]ce [eye] t must [be] an act of kindness [to] in [form] the [coin]less how they [may] reinforce their [purse] [eye] w[ill] acquaint [all] with the t[rue] secret of [money] [cat]ching the certain way [to] fill empty [purses] & how [to] keep them [al]ways full. Two simple [rules] [well] observed w[ill] do the bus[i]ness 1st Let ho[nest]y and [industry] [bee] thy const[ant] comp[an]ions 2d S[pen]d one [penny] every day less than thy cl[ear] gains [then] [shall] thy [purse] soon [be]gin to thr[i]ve, thy cred[i]tors will n[eve]r insult thee nor w[ant] op[press] nor hunger [bite] e nor [nakedness] freeze thee, the whole hemi[sphere] will sh[i]ne [brig]hter and pleasure sp[ring] up in every [corn]er of thy [heart]. Now thereby emb[race] these [rules] and [bee] Happy.

B Franklin

"The Art of Making Money Plenty" from the *Almanack*. Can you read Ben's message?

Franklin at age 20

Fire Department Hose Carriage

which came from the 1735 almanac. To describe a long-winded minister, people might say, "As Poor Richard says, *A good example is the best sermon*," which came from the 1747 almanac.

The thousands of people who eagerly awaited Franklin's 1750 almanac were not disappointed. That year his witty sayings included "Genius without education is like silver in the mine" and "Little strokes fell great oaks." Poor Richard especially liked to tell people how to make and keep money, and in the 1751 almanac he came up with the saying "Time is money."

In addition to his publishing ventures, Ben Franklin was famous for improving the city in many ways. In 1731, he had founded the Library Company of Philadelphia, the colonies' first library to circulate books. Five years later he had founded the thirteen colonies' first volunteer fire department. In 1751, the year the academy opened, Franklin helped start the Pennsylvania Hospital, the country's first general hospital. People wondered how Ben Franklin could do so much around the city and still find time for his electrical experiments and a growing political career in the Pennsylvania Assembly.

By today's standards, 1750 Philadelphia was a small town, but it was home to many people who are now famous. One was seventy-six-year-old James Logan, who had come to Pennsylvania in 1699 with William Penn and had served as mayor of Philadelphia, chief justice of the Pennsylvania Supreme Court, and acting governor of Pennsylvania. Also, there was six-year-old Thomas Mifflin, who would later sign the U.S. Constitution. On New Year's Day, 1752, a baby girl named Betsy Griscom was born in Philadelphia. Later, when her married name was Betsy Ross, she would become famous for her work on the first United States flag.

James Logan

They didn't have TV, radio, or movies, but the Philadelphians of 1750 knew how to have fun. Men liked to spend their evenings playing cards and talking to their friends in taverns. Billiards and bowling were popular with the men, too, as was horse racing. Organized horse races were held on what is now Race Street, but some young lawbreakers held their own challenge races on the city's busy streets. Philadelphia women enjoyed visiting with friends and relatives, and also gardening. Dancing was popular among both women and men.

Families went to watch the acrobats and tight-rope walkers who came to town from time to time.

Thomas Mifflin

Showmen who traveled about exhibiting giraffes, leopards, and other wild animals were quite successful since few colonists had seen such creatures before.

Also, a steady stream of philosophers and traveling preachers came to Philadelphia. One of them who claimed he could walk on the Delaware River proved to be all wet, but Philadelphians enjoyed what he and the other traveling speakers had to say about the world's future and the best way to save one's soul.

The Quakers considered the theater a waste of time, but by 1750, acting companies occasionally visited Philadelphia. One group performed a number of plays including Shakespeare's *Richard III* in a warehouse in 1749–1750. A troupe that arrived in 1754 performed *Miss in Her Teens* and other plays. Wealthy Philadelphians also enjoyed having their portraits done by the city's artists.

Philadelphia in the mid-1700s was in the process of growing from a small town into a real city. Many new buildings were going up, and even the State House (capitol building) was being improved. From 1750 to 1753 Philadelphians watched as a tower was built on the State House. In 1751, the Pennsylvania Assembly decided that a bell should be placed in the new tower to celebrate the fiftieth anniversary of William Penn's Charter of Privileges. An order for a one ton bell was placed with a foundry in England. Because William Penn had planned his colony as a place of liberty, the Biblical words PROCLAIM LIBERTY THROUGHOUT ALL THE LAND UNTO ALL THE INHABITANTS THEREOF were to be inscribed on the bell.

The Liberty Bell

The ship carrying the bell arrived in Philadelphia in August of 1752. The tower was not yet finished, so the bell was taken to the State House yard for testing. As soon as it was rung, however, the bell cracked. Two ironworkers recast the huge bell, which was placed in the tower in 1753.

As they watched it being raised to the State House tower, the Philadelphians of 1753 would have been surprised to know that the bell would one day become a symbol of America, and that it would even appear on some of the nation's coins. After being rung at many historic occasions, including the adoption of the Declaration of Independence, it became known as the Liberty Bell. And because the Declaration of Independence was adopted there, the State House became known as Independence Hall.

Rivers were crossed by rope ferry

LIFE IN THE PENNSYLVANIA COUNTRYSIDE

Philadelphia was home to only 15,000 of the 120,000 colonists who lived in Pennsylvania in 1750. The other 105,000 colonists lived in smaller towns and on scattered farms. Although families were slowly pushing into the other three-fourths of Pennsylvania, as of 1750 southeastern Pennsylvania was still by far the colony's most popular region.

Lancaster, which had been founded in 1718, was Pennsylvania's second-largest town by 1750 with about two thousand people. Other towns in southeastern Pennsylvania that had been founded by 1750 included York, Reading, Bethlehem, and Germantown (now part of Philadelphia). Carlisle, near the present capital city of Harrisburg, was laid out in 1751, but Harrisburg itself wasn't laid out by John Harris, Jr., until 1785.

First house built in Bethlehem, 1741

People had various reasons for living in the countryside rather than in Philadelphia. Several of the religious groups wanted to create their own communities outside the big city. For example, the group called the Amish believed that farming was the proper pursuit of humanity, so they had built farming communities outside Philadelphia. The Moravians had founded the town of Bethlehem, which today is one of the main headquarters of the Moravian Church. The Mennonites had founded Germantown, and later had settled in other parts of southeastern Pennsylvania.

The countryside also attracted quite a few ex-indentured servants. These people had worked for several years to repay persons who had paid for their passage to America. Once their term of service was over, the ex-indentured servants were ready to start homes of their own. What better place to do this than the Pennsylvania frontier, where there was plenty of land available?

As is still true today, there were also many colonists who disliked the "crowding" in Philadelphia and other cities and preferred the wide open spaces. Some of these people would move to an area, live there a while, and then go off to a new unsettled region as soon as a few neighbors arrived. Those who sought more "elbow-room" on the Pennsylvania frontier came from the Philadelphia area, from Europe, and also from Virginia, Maryland, New Jersey, and Connecticut.

Upon arriving at the site of their new home with their cow and their few belongings, the pioneer family chopped down trees, made them into logs, and then built a log cabin. To keep rain and cold out of their cabin, the family filled the cracks with moss or mud. Sometimes a few friends and relatives settled together in an area. Where this occurred, there might soon be a new town.

The pioneer family planted crops such as corn, wheat, rye, potatoes, peas, and flax. All but the flax provided food. (Flax fibers were used to make cloth.) More food was brought home by the father who hunted deer, elk, bears, and wild turkeys. Frontier mothers sometimes shot wild animals that wandered near their log cabins.

The mother and older daughters prepared the food. Many poorer families ate an instant pudding called cornmeal mush every day of the year. Johnnycake, a bread made with cornmeal, was also popular. The vegetables grown on the farm and the meat brought home from the forest were made into tasty soups and stews. For special treats, frontier women made pies out of the raspberries, strawberries, and cherries that they gathered.

Water was not a popular drink in colonial days because if it was impure it often transmitted diseases. Many families owned cows which provided them with milk. It was also quite common for everyone in the family—even children—to drink whiskey, which the colonists made out of corn, rye, wheat, and barley. The whiskey was often mixed with spices, milk, and sugar, which many people thought improved the taste.

Some frontier families bought their clothes in Philadelphia or in other towns, but many made their clothes themselves. This was especially true of people who lived far away from any sizable town. Deerskin was used to make breeches (pants), shirts, jackets, and moccasins. From their flax crops the colonists made a cloth called linen, which was used to make petticoats, gowns, aprons, shirts, and also tablecloths and sheets.

To dye their clothes, the pioneers used forest products. Many of their clothes were dull yellow because that was the color of the popular dye made from butternut tree bark. A red dye was

Frontiersman wears a shirt, pants, and moccasins made of deerskin.

made from the roots of the madder herb, and the hulls of black walnuts yielded a brown dye.

The frontier Pennsylvanians of 1750 lived to an average age of twenty-five. Although some lived to seventy and eighty, many children died of disease during their first five years. The people were so desperate for medicines that they thought up a number of odd-sounding remedies. For example, some tried to cure epilepsy by eating rattlesnake hearts, while others tried to cure kidney trouble by drinking goat urine. There was a widespread belief that if a medicine was disgusting enough, it could drive off the disease.

Families living close to a town dressed in their nicest clothes on Sunday and walked or rode to church. Those living far from a town sometimes gathered in a neighbor's cabin and held their own services. Log churches with log pews and a log pulpit were also built in some wilderness areas. Local people or traveling ministers held the services in these frontier churches.

A traveling preacher

Schools were much rarer than churches on the frontier. There were a few schools for the wealthy young people in the towns, but by adulthood most frontier Pennsylvanians had received less schooling than the average second grader of today. The only book owned by many families was the Bible, with which parents used to teach their children reading skills and religious lessons. The only other education many children received was a little basic arithmetic.

Despite their lack of education, frontier Pennsylvanians were responsible for two of the most important inventions in American history: the "Kentucky rifle" and the Conestoga wagon. Both were created in the Lancaster area.

By the early 1700s, the finest rifles in the world were called *jaegers*, which had originated in central Europe. German colonists brought jaegers with them when they settled in the Lancaster region. Once there, they created new versions of these guns, with longer barrels and other improved features. These new guns were the best rifles ever made up to that time. Because they had been first made in Pennsylvania, they should have been called "Pennsylvania rifles." But because Kentucky was the general name for frontier America at the time, and because Pennsylvania-born Daniel Boone used them when he helped settle Kentucky, these weapons became known as "Kentucky rifles."

By 1750, thousands of frontier Pennsylvanians owned Kentucky rifles, which Lancaster-area gunsmiths sold for about twenty dollars each. Many men and teenaged boys became such crack shots with these rifles that they could hit small targets repeatedly at four hundred feet. These lightweight rifles were used for hunting and for shooting contests, and later many American soldiers used them against the British during the Revolutionary War.

Incredibly, at the same time that Lancaster-area

gunsmiths were creating "Kentucky rifles," wagon-makers in the same region were revolutionizing transportation. The farmers around Lancaster wanted a sturdy wagon that could handle bumpy roads and cross rivers. In response, the German wagon-makers created a sturdy canvas-covered wagon that weighed about three thousand pounds, had removable wheels so that it could be floated across streams, and was usually pulled by six horses. These wagons were called Conestoga wagons because they were invented

Conestoga wagons on the Lancaster Pike

near Conestoga Creek in the Lancaster, Pennsylvania, region.

By 1750, Conestoga wagons were regularly traveling between Philadelphia and Lancaster over what was called the Conestoga Road. For about a century, Conestoga wagons were the main vehicles used to take goods over mountainous roads in America. Some of the Conestoga wagon drivers smoked long, thin cigars that were called *stogies*, from the word Cone*stoga*. To this day, some people call cigars *stogies*. The Conestoga wagon drivers were also said to have originated the American custom of driving on the right side of the road.

Daniel Boone

A number of people who would one day become famous lived in the Pennsylvania countryside. Daniel Boone, who became colonial America's most famous frontiersman, lived his first sixteen years in rural Pennsylvania. However, in 1750, he and his family went off to North Carolina seeking more "elbow-room." In 1750, eighteen-year-old David Rittenhouse, who was to become a famous astronomer and first director of the U.S. Mint, was living at his father's farm a few miles outside Philadelphia.

BENJAMIN FRANKLIN (1706-1790)

Born on Milk Street in Boston, Benjamin Franklin was the fifteenth in a family of seventeen children. He was probably taught to read by his family, but when telling his life story years later, Franklin wrote that he couldn't remember a time when he did not know how to read. Ben also began his inventing career early. To make swimming easier, he built paddles which he tied to his feet and hands. He also held on to the string of an airborne kite, then floated on his back and let the kite pull him through the water!

Ben Franklin's father, who made candles and soap in his Milk Street shop, wanted Ben to study for the ministry at Harvard College, near Boston. But it turned out that the Franklins could not afford a college education for Ben. As a result, he had just two years of formal schooling, between the ages of eight and ten.

Benjamin Franklin examines his newest invention, bifocal glasses

Mr. Franklin then began grooming Ben to one day take over his shop, but the ten-year-old boy hated making candles. What he loved was reading books and then writing essays in which he imitated his favorite authors. Realizing that Ben would be better at making words than candles and soap, Mr. Franklin decided that he should become a printer. At twelve, Ben signed up to serve as apprentice to his own older brother, James, who was a printer.

Under James Franklin's guidance, Ben became an expert printer. In 1721, James began the *New England Courant*, one of the early newspapers in the American colonies. Ben decided to write some articles for the paper, but he didn't want James to know about it. Disguising his handwriting, Ben wrote some articles under the name Silence Dogwood, and slipped them under the print-shop door late at night. The Silence Dogwood articles became popular around Boston, but James was angry when he learned that they had been written by his younger brother.

In 1722, James was jailed for a month because British authorities were upset about something he had printed. Although only sixteen at the time, Ben ran the paper for the month. James was released from jail under the order that he stop publishing the *New England Courant*. Ben was then named the paper's publisher, with the understanding that James would secretly give the orders. Ben had ideas of his own about the newspaper business, though, and the brothers often fought. Sometimes, James even beat up Ben. When he was seventeen, Ben decided to go off on his own.

Out of spite, James Franklin kept Ben from finding another printing job in Boston. Ben then sold some of his books and went to New York City. He couldn't find work there, either, so he headed to Philadelphia. Ben walked most of the last fifty miles to Philadelphia, arriving on a Sunday morning wet, hungry, and with only about a dollar in his pocket. Entering

Philadelphia, Ben was spotted by Deborah Read who happened to be standing in her doorway. Deborah laughed at Ben's weather-beaten appearance, but later they were married for forty-four years.

Ben landed a job with a Philadelphia printer and did very well. By twenty-two, he had his own printing firm and soon after that he was publishing his own newspaper, the *Pennsylvania Gazette*. In 1733, he began publishing his very successful *Poor Richard's Almanack*.

Although Poor Richard claimed that "Early to bed and early to rise, makes a man healthy, wealthy, and wise," Ben Franklin didn't follow that advice! After working as a printer and publisher all day, he often stayed up late reading books on many subjects, performing scientific experiments, and working with people to improve Philadelphia.

Franklin achieved more in more fields than any other American ever. As an inventor, he created bifocal glasses, the lightning rod, the Franklin stove (a heating device), an early odometer (a device for measuring distances), and one of the first rocking chairs. Saying that he was happy to help people, Franklin refused to make money from his inventions.

As a scientist, he became famous for his experiments with electricity. In summer of 1752, near what is now Race and Eighth streets in Philadelphia, he flew a homemade kite in a storm. Suddenly a lightning bolt zoomed down the kite string to a key, where it made a spark. This highly dangerous experiment proved that lightning is electricity. Franklin also studied ocean currents and population growth. And he suggested the plate tectonic theory (which explains the causes of earthquakes and volcanoes) two centuries before it was accepted by geologists.

As a public servant, Ben founded America's first general hospital, its first volunteer fire department, its first library that circulated books, and the University of Pennsylvania.

Franklin made his greatest contributions to his country during the Revolutionary War era. When troubles began with Britain, he tried to keep America in the British Empire, but by 1775, he strongly supported American independence. He was the only person to sign all of these four vital documents in early United States history: the Declaration of Independence, the Alliance with France, the peace treaty with Britain, and the United States Constitution. Without the help that Franklin obtained from France, the United states might have lost the war.

Even at the most serious of times, Ben Franklin often kept his humor. During the signing of the Declaration of Independence, John Hancock supposedly said that the delegates must "all hang together," meaning that they must cooperate. Franklin was said to have answered, "We must all hang together, or assuredly we shall all hang separately!" One of the great figures of American and also world history, Benjamin Franklin died in Philadelphia at the age of eighty-four.

Franklin's Electrostatic Machine used for experimenting with electricity between 1746 and 1749

Indians gather for a
surprise attack during
the French and Indian
War

Chapter VII

The French and Indian War (1754–1763)

You know very well, when the white people came first here, they were poor; but now they have got our lands, and are by them become rich, and we are now poor. What little we had for the land goes soon away, but the land lasts forever.

Sachradadow, a Cayuga Indian chief, speaking at a meeting at Lancaster, Pennsylvania during the early 1700s

By the mid-1700s, the remaining Indians in Pennsylvania were very angry about being cheated out of their lands. The Indians had generously allowed the Europeans to colonize southeastern Pennsylvania, but they had not expected the settlers to eventually take *all* the land. By 1753, the Indians had not only been swindled out of their homelands by the Walking Purchase and other treaties, but settlers were even living on lands that still belonged to the Indians. Many of the Delaware Indians had been pushed all the way into western Pennsylvania.

Few of the colonists knew or cared about the promises that William Penn had made to the Indians seventy years earlier. They only cared about the angry Indians making frontier life dangerous. Many colonists thought that the only way to deal with these hostile Indians was through the barrel of a Kentucky rifle.

Meanwhile, Great Britain and France had been fighting on and off since the late 1600s over North American lands. Both countries were interested in seizing control of what is now the central United States. Also, Britain wanted France's Canadian holdings, while the French wanted the thirteen British colonies.

Between 1689 and 1748, Britain and France fought three wars over North American lands. The three were called King William's War (1689–1697), Queen Anne's War (1702–1713), and King George's War (1744–1748). These three struggles did not settle the issue. The dispute was only ended by the French and Indian War, which was waged between 1754 and 1763.

The French had been friendly with the Indians for a long time and were more interested in trading with them than in seizing their lands as the British had done. For these reasons most

Indians who fought in the French and Indian War sided with France. The name *French and Indian War* is misleading, though, because although more Indians fought for France, some did side with Britain. On one side of the struggle were the British, the colonists, and their Indian allies. On the other side were the French, their larger number of Indian friends, and some Canadians.

Since the colonists and the British rulers in Pennsylvania had mistreated the Indians for decades, most of the Delawares and the other Native Americans of the region sided with France. A great deal of the fighting took place in Pennsylvania, including the opening battle.

In 1753, the French built several forts in what is now western Pennsylvania. At what is now Erie near the state's northwest corner, they built Fort Presque Isle, and nearby, where the town of Waterford now stands, they built Fort Le Boeuf.

At the time, the Virginia Colony claimed western Pennsylvania, and so the Virginia governor, Robert Dinwiddie, decided to ask the French to leave the region. A twenty-one-year-old Virginia major named George Washington volunteered to take the message to the French.

Washington set out from Virginia in fall of 1753. On the way to Pennsylvania, Washington was joined by several frontiersmen, including the famous guide and explorer Christopher Gist. After a difficult journey lasting several weeks, the men reached Fort Le Boeuf in northwestern Pennsylvania in December. Washington gave Governor Dinwiddie's message to the French commander, Legardeur de St. Pierre, but he politely refused to withdraw his country's forces.

While heading back to Virginia with Gist, the man who would later become "The Father of His Country" had a couple of brushes with death in Pennsylvania. Once a supposedly friendly Indian turned and fired his gun at the two men, fortunately missing. Another time the two travelers were crossing the icy Allegheny River on a raft when Washington was suddenly thrown into the freezing water. He managed to pull himself back onto the log raft, but it went out of control. Just when it seemed that the two men would die in the frigid river, they reached a little island. That night the temperature dropped so low that the river froze completely, enabling them to walk across it the next morning.

By mid-January, Washington was back in Virginia. He gave Governor Dinwiddie the French answer, then advised him to build a fort at the place where the Ohio and Allegheny rivers meet.

Dinwiddie sent out a force to construct the fort, which was the start of the city of Pittsburgh.

In spring ot 1754, Governor Dinwiddie sent Washington out with more than 150 soldiers to defend the new fort. When still several hundred miles from the fort, however, Washington learned that it had been captured by French soldiers. The French had begun building their own army post, which they called Fort Duquesne, also on the site where Pittsburgh now stands.

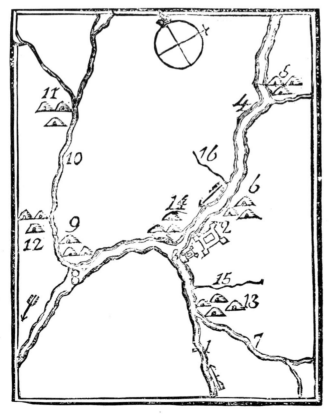

French army post Fort Duquesne and surrounding territory

Key:
1. Monongahela River
2. Fort Duquesne, or Pittsburgh
3. Small fort
4. Alleghany River
5. Alleghany Indian town
6. Shanapins
7. Yauyaugany River
8. Ohio, or Alleghany River
9. Logs Town
10. Beaver Creek
11. Kuskaskies
12. Shingoes Town
13. Alleguippes
14. Sennakaas
15. Tuttle Creek
16. Pine Creek
Arrows show the course of the river.

Washington at Fort Duquesne

Washington led some of his men toward Fort Duquesne. At dawn of May 28, 1754, Washington and his forces made a surprise attack on French troops at a place called Great Meadows near what is now Uniontown, Pennsylvania. Washington's soldiers killed the French leader and nine of his troops, and captured over twenty others. The Battle of Great Meadows was the first battle of the French and Indian War.

Not far from where they had won the Battle of Great Meadows, Washington and his men built their own outpost, which they called Fort Necessity. The French had many more troops in the area than the British, though, and on July 3, 1754, a French force of about 1,000 men began firing on George Washington and his 400 men inside Fort Necessity. Washington's forces fired back, killing and wounding several hundred of the enemy. But after a hundred of his own men had been killed or wounded by French gunfire, and seeing that supplies were low, Washington decided to surrender. He and his men were allowed to march out of the fort and leave Pennsylvania. This big French victory meant that the French were now in total control of western Pennsylvania.

General Edward Braddock

When British lawmakers in London learned of this defeat, they decided to send a thousand soldiers to Pennsylvania under General Edward Braddock. The general and his men arrived in Virginia in early 1755.

Braddock asked the colonies to provide money for him to pay his soldiers. In Pennsylvania the war-hating Quakers controlled the Assembly, and they offered little help. However, Ben Franklin eventually convinced the Pennsylvania Assembly to provide funds for defense and arranged for the colony to provide Braddock with 150 Conestoga wagons and hundreds of horses.

General Braddock assembled his supplies at Fort Cumberland (now the city of Cumberland), Maryland. In addition to the thousand men he had brought from Britain, Braddock was joined by several hundred colonial troops. Braddock had heard about George Washington, and he invited the young American soldier to serve as his aide.

The British general's first goal was to capture Fort Duquesne from the French. Braddock could have done that, but his own personality stood in his way. He insultingly referred to the colonial troops as "raw American militia," and even turned away many Indians who had offered to join his side. Braddock predicted that the Fench and the "savages" who were aiding them would be easily beaten by his troops.

Nearly a hundred miles of rough ground separated Fort Cumberland, Maryland, and Fort Duquesne, Pennsylvania. The Braddock expedition set out on June 7, 1755. At the front of the

Braddock's march to Fort Duquesne

expedition, lumberjacks blazed a trail through the wilderness. Following the woodchoppers was a four-mile-long procession of marching soldiers, Conestoga wagons, horses, cannons, and the large coach carrying General Braddock.

Indians who saw the expedition cutting through the forest reported the news to the

French at Fort Duquesne. After a month of moving at a rate of three miles per day, the Braddock expedition came within a few miles of Fort Duquesne on July 9. Braddock ordered his men to make camp, and then began planning to attack the fort the next day.

Meanwhile, the French commander at Fort Duquesne, Captain Hyacinthe de Beaujeu, realized that he could not stop the British assault. For one thing, the British had about 1,400 men compared to the 300 French and Canadian soldiers within Fort Duquesne and the several hundred Indians camped outside the fort. Also, the British cannons were capable of blowing Fort Duquesne to smithereens.

Beaujeu decided that the best strategy was to fight the British before they could set up their cannons. He led several hundred French and Canadian soldiers and Indians to the British encampment.

Braddock and Thomas Gage, who was one of his officers, had failed to protect their troops from just such an ambush. Hiding behind trees, the French forces suddenly fired upon the startled British troops.

To understand how the outmanned French defeated the British, it helps to know a little about the warfare of the time. Most European generals thought it was "ungentlemanly" to make sneak attacks or fight from a hiding place. The French, though, had learned from their Indian friends that these were effective techniques for fighting in the American wilderness. The French did this at the Battle of the Wilderness, as it was called, and that was why they won.

Early in the battle, the French commander Hyacinthe de Beaujeu was killed, but the French kept firing from their hiding places. Braddock's soldiers begged to be allowed to fight from behind trees, too. Washington, who himself had made a surprise dawn attack at Great Meadows, also asked Braddock to let the men fight from behind trees. Braddock refused. Screaming "Cowards!" he even hit some of his men with his sword when they left their positions.

Washington later said that he had barely escaped death many times during the Battle of the Wilderness, which was fought in south-western Pennsylvania on July 9, 1755. "I had four bullets through my coat and two horses shot under me," he later wrote. Not so lucky were 800 others on the British side, who were either killed outright or wounded. In those days, most soldiers who were hurt badly enough to be listed as "wounded" died from the wounds or from infection.

Four horses were shot out from under the sixty-year-old Edward Braddock, who fought very bravely. As the general mounted the fifth horse, he was shot in the chest, possibly by one of his own men who was angry at him for making them fight out in the open. "Who would have thought it?" the badly-wounded Braddock mumbled, after this terrible British defeat. The next day his condition worsened. "We shall better know how to deal with them another time," he said, and then died a few minutes later.

For several years after the Battle of the Wilderness, it appeared that France would win the French and Indian War. The French won several important battles in the New York region. And during their many raids on Pennsylvania's frontier settlements, the Indians on the French side scalped colonists, took prisoners, and burned log cabins.

Pennsylvania Governor Robert Hunter Morris and his Council struck back at the Indians in the cruelest way. They offered the colonists a large reward for "the scalp of every male Indian enemy above the age of twelve years." These officials hated the Indians so much that they were encouraging people to kill twelve-year-old boys. The Pennsylvania Assembly took a more reasonable approach by building, under Ben Franklin's guidance, dozens of forts to protect the frontier people.

Pennsylvania Governor Robert Hunter Morris

Meanwhile, British lawmakers decided to increase the number of men and weapons for the war effort. In 1758, Britain sent a nearly 8,000-man army to Philadelphia under General John Forbes. Forbes's orders were to proceed to Fort Duquesne and seize it from the French. Just as Braddock had done, Forbes took Washington along with him.

At first it appeared that Forbes's expedition might fail as badly as Braddock's. In September of 1758, Forbes sent out an advance party of about eight hundred men to scout the Fort Duquesne area. The leader of the scouting party, Major James Grant, disobeyed orders by marching his men too close to the fort. The French and the Indians rushed out of Fort Duquesne and attacked the British troops, killing over three hundred of them. In November, though, Forbes's main army approached Fort Duquesne. Seeing that the British army was much larger than theirs, the French blew up Fort Duquesne and then headed for Canada.

General Forbes had his men build a new army post near the site of Fort Duquesne. The new fort was named Fort Pitt, for the famous British statesman William Pitt. Forbes named the town that grew up around the fort *Pittsburgh*. Today,

Blockhouse at Fort Pitt (left) and plan of Fort Pitt (right)

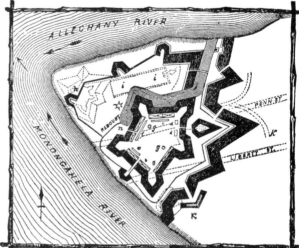

Pittsburgh is the second-largest city in Pennsylvania, after Philadelphia.

The British had other successes on the battlefield. In 1758–1759, they won several major battles in Canada and in New York. Then in September of 1759, the British won the war's decisive battle at Quebec, Canada. Although the fighting continued for a short while, the British victory at the Battle of Quebec meant that Britain and not France would have control of much of North America. According to the peace treaty that was signed in 1763, Canada and all French possessions east of the Mississippi River except New Orleans passed into British control.

In Pennsylvania, the Indians continued to fight the settlers even after the French and Indian War ended. The Ottawa Chief Pontiac organized an army that included Delaware, Ottawa, Seneca, and Shawnee Indians. In spring of 1763, this Indian confederacy began attacking frontier settlements between Pittsburgh, Pennsylvania, and Detroit, Michigan. The Indians captured several forts in Pennsylvania, and nearly won Fort Pitt. Pontiac's War ended soon after Colonel Henry Bouquet and his 500 men defeated the Indians at the Battle of Bushy Run, fought near Greensburg, Pennsylvania, in August of 1763.

Chief Pontiac

British soldiers watch as Indians leave a fort in Detroit.

One of the most tragic events in Pennsylvania history took place several months after the Battle of Bushy Run. The Pennsylvania government had allowed the settlers to organize groups of Rangers to fight hostile Indians. In the Harrisburg area there was a group of Rangers known as the "Paxton Boys." These Indian-haters decided that all Indians, even friendly ones, must leave Pennsylvania. At the time, the last twenty Susquehannock Indians in the world were living peacefully in the Indian village at Conestoga, near Lancaster. The rest of the Susquehannocks had been wiped out by war and disease.

When those last twenty Susquehannocks would not leave Pennsylvania, the Paxton Boys marched to Conestoga in mid-December of 1763 and murdered six of them. Fourteen other Susquehannocks who had been away from home learned about the massacre and took refuge in the jail in nearby Lancaster. A Mennonite who heard the Paxton Boys threatening to kill the remaining Susquehannocks told officials about it, but they ignored him.

Two days after Christmas of 1763, the Paxton Boys broke into the Lancaster jail and murdered those last fourteen Susquehannocks—mostly old men, women, and children. The Paxton Boys then marched toward Philadelphia, intending to kill a hundred Indians who had gone there for safety. Benjamin Franklin, who referred to the Paxton Boys as "white savages," helped convince them to leave the Indians alone and return home.

By the late 1760s, most of the surviving Delawares and other Indians who had once lived in Pennsylvania had gone to live in Ohio and other places.* By the late 1700s, only about a thousand Indians were left in Pennsylvania.

* For more information about Indians see page 152

To protest taxes, the colonists burned the Stamp Act papers.

Chapter VIII

The Revolutionary War

*When in the Course of human events, it becomes
necessary for one people to dissolve the political
bands which have connected them with another,
and to assume among the powers of the earth, the
separate and equal station to which the Laws of
Nature and of Nature's God entitle them, a decent
respect to the opinions of mankind requires that
they should declare the causes which impel them to
the separation.*

> *Beginning of the American Declaration of
> Independence, adopted in Philadelphia on
> July 4, 1776*

Great Britain had money problems after
winning the French and Indian War. The cost of
the war had been astronomical. There had been
soldiers to pay, forts and ships to build, and
cannons, guns, and uniforms to buy. Britain had
not been able to pay all its expenses during the
war, so when the fighting ended, the country had
a huge debt. In addition, Britain had to protect its
North American empire from possible attack by
the French or other enemies. To provide this
costly protection, Britain sent several thousand
troops to North America.

In London the British lawmaking body, *Parliament*, discussed how to raise more money. Parliament decided that the American colonists should pay a good portion of it, especially since much of the debt had come from trying to protect them.

Starting in 1764, Parliament passed one act after another taxing the colonists. There were taxes on sugar, tea, paper, wine, cloth, and other items. Few people are happy about paying taxes, but what enraged the colonists most was the fact that they had not been given a say in making these new tax laws. They agreed with famed British statesman William Pitt who said, "No subject of England shall be taxed but by his own consent." The colonists coined a slogan of their own—"Taxation without representation is tyranny!" In other words, since they were not allowed to send representatives to Parliament, they thought Parliament had no right to tax them.

One tax that was despised throughout the thirteen colonies was called the Stamp Act. It required that the colonists buy special stamps to be placed on newspapers, wills, and various legal documents. The Stamp Act was to go into effect on November 1, 1765, but there were protests

Tax Stamp

against the act throughout the colonies. Men calling themselves "Sons of Liberty" even tarred and feathered some British stamp officials.

Surprised by the intensity of the Americans' anger, the Parliament repealed the Stamp Act early in 1766. When this news reached America in spring of 1766, celebrations were held throughout the colonies. In Philadelphia, bonfires were lit, cannons were fired from the State House yard, and the city's bells, including the Liberty Bell, were rung.

Britain was not ready to let the Americans have their way about everything, though. In fact, the government decided that the colonists had to become more obedient. That was why, after repealing the Stamp Act, Parliament passed a law stating that the colonists had to obey British laws "in all cases whatsoever."

But, as they had done with the Stamp Act, Americans continued to disobey the tax laws that they considered unjust. They struck back by refusing to buy British goods. Women (the main purchasers of household goods) and men either bought goods made in non-British countries or they made things themselves. For example, many colonists dressed in homespun clothes instead of

Colonists hang representations of Stamp tax officials

buying British garments. As a result, instead of
getting more money out of the colonists, Britain
received less.

Anger over the tax laws wasn't the sole reason
that the colonists were turning against the
mother country. By 1770, about two out of five
colonists were of non-English heritage. This
meant that of the 2,000,000 colonists in America,
about 800,000 were of Scottish, Irish, Scotch-
Irish, German, Swedish, Swiss, Dutch, and French
ancestry. Large numbers of these people felt little

or no loyalty to England, and many even hated the country. For example, Ireland had been oppressed by England for centuries, so many Irish Americans despised England.

There was also a widespread feeling that Britain had not provided enough help during the French and Indian War. Having fought to save their homes and towns, people felt that they deserved more of a say in governing themselves.

Finally, there was a growing sentiment that the colonists had created a new nationality. No matter where they had come from, the American colonists had more in common with each other than with the people in the "old country." They shared problems concerning farming and town-building. Most of them dressed and spoke similarly. They married each other, too, and later had children who were a blend of many back-grounds but thought of themselves as Americans.

In the late 1760s and early 1770s the colonists protested and rioted so violently against the British injustices that the mother country shipped in soldiers to keep order. Americans hated being monitored by these soldiers, whom they called "lobsterbacks" or "bloodybacks" because of their red uniforms. The Sons of Liberty and neighborhood children pelted the soldiers with snowballs and rocks. For revenge, the soldiers sometimes cut down the patriots' "liberty poles"—trees under which they gathered for protest meetings.

After the redcoats damaged their liberty pole, the New York City Sons of Liberty fought with about sixty British soldiers at Golden Hill. A number of patriots were stabbed with bayonets and some soldiers were beaten up in this brawl, which is known as the Battle of Golden Hill. Two months later, on March 5, 1770, a group of Bostonians threw stones at some British soldiers, who then fired into the crowd, killing five people. Although the colonists had started this brawl, the Boston patriot Samuel Adams called it the "Boston Massacre."

Boston was the hub of American unrest. On December 16, 1773, about fifty Bostonians boarded three British ships and tossed 340 chests of tea into Boston Harbor to protest the tax on tea. Britain ordered Bostonians to pay for this "Boston Tea Party," but they refused, and in June of 1774, Britain closed Boston's port as punishment. The ban on ships entering or leaving their harbor caused much hardship for Bostonians, but people in other colonies sent food and supplies to the city.

Boston Massacre, March 5, 1770

Sam Adams of Massachusetts and Ben Franklin of Pennsylvania suggested that representatives from all the colonies meet to discuss the troubles with Britain. It was decided that this congress of colonial leaders would meet in Philadelphia, Penn-

A meeting of the First Continental Congress in Philadelphia's Carpenters' Hall

sylvania, in fall of 1774. The First Continental Congress, as it was called, opened in Philadelphia's Carpenters' Hall on September 5, 1774. From that day on, Pennsylvania played a leading role in the creation of the United States.

Georgia sent no delegates to the First Continental Congress, but agreed to abide by Congress's decisions. The other twelve colonies sent a total of fifty-six delegates. Among the seven who represented Pennsylvania were John Dickinson, Joseph Galloway, and Thomas Mifflin.

John Dickinson

There was little talk of revolution at that First Continental Congress. Most of the delegates simply wanted fairer treatment rather than a break from Britain. But in case it came to war, the Congress told the colonies to arm themselves and form emergency military forces called *militia*. The Congress also approved a Declaration of Rights of Americans, sent petitions to Britain asking for fairer treatment, and planned a boycott of British products. The First Continental Congress closed on October 26, 1774, after meeting for two months. The delegates planned to hold another meeting in the spring if British lawmakers failed to meet their demands.

Militia groups were created in many colonial towns in 1774 and 1775. Some units became known as *minutemen* because they claimed they could be ready to fight in a minute. The minutemen and the other militia practiced marching and shooting. They also hid large supplies of weapons in barns and houses in case

Joseph Galloway

they needed them.

As expected, British lawmakers refused to accept the Americans' demands. To decide what to do next, the Second Continental Congress planned to meet in Philadelphia again in May of 1775. But just three weeks before this meeting was scheduled to start, American militia units fought British troops at Lexington and Concord—two Massachusetts towns a few miles northwest of Boston.

On the night of April 18, 1775, General Thomas Gage sent British troops out of Boston. Gage's goals were to capture the American leaders Sam Adams and John Hancock in Lexington and then to seize gunpowder in Concord.

Boston patriots learned that the British were marching toward Lexington. Boston silversmith Paul Revere warned Sam Adams and John Hancock that the British were coming, and the two leaders fled Lexington. As church bells tolled, the town's minutemen gathered on Lexington's village green.

About seventy-five minutemen were waiting for the British when they arrived at Lexington green at dawn of April 19, 1775. The minutemen had guns, but they were farmers, not soldiers, and

General Thomas Gage

there were quite a few teenaged boys and old men among them. The war did not begin well for the Americans. When the British Major John Pitcairn ordered them to put down their guns, the outnumbered colonists ran for home. Suddenly someone fired a shot—no one knows from which side. The British then shot down the helpless minutemen, killing eight of them and wounding ten, while having only one man wounded themselves. The Battle of Lexington, which was the first battle of the American Revolution, was a complete British victory.

Battle of Lexington was the first battle of the American Revolution.

News about the battle spread, and as the redcoats headed toward Concord, minutemen from across the Massachusetts countryside headed there, too. The Americans gathered more men than the British at Concord, and this time when the redcoats fired at them hundreds of the patriots fired back. The patriots outfought the British at Concord, then chased them back toward Boston. During their retreat, the redcoats tried to march in an orderly manner, but the Americans kept pace and shot at them from behind trees, just as the French had done at the Battle of the Wilderness twenty years earlier. The minutemen picked off the redcoats as if they were targets in a shooting contest. This running Battle of Concord was the first American victory of the revolution. By the time the British reached Boston, nearly three hundred redcoats had been killed or wounded, while the patriots had suffered about a hundred casualties.

Three weeks after these battles, the Second Continental Congress opened at the Pennsylvania State House in Philadelphia. This time, Benjamin Franklin was one of the Pennsylvania delegates to the Congress.

Few people realize it today, but even after the Battles of Lexington and Concord, most

Americans hoped that the dispute with Britain would be settled peacefuly. Dating back to the 1600s, there had been armed fights between the Americans and the British without war developing. The Battles of Lexington and Concord were far more serious than any of these previous struggles, but many people still felt that things could be patched up, if only Britain would back down.

When the Second Continental Congress opened in the Pennsylvania State House on May 10, 1775, there still weren't very many delegates who were ready to declare America independent of Britain. Soon after convening, Congress even sent a letter to King George asking that "harmony between [Britain] and these Colonies may be restored." Written by Pennsylvania delegate John Dickinson, this paper was called the "Olive Branch Petition" because the olive branch has long been a symbol of peace.

But harmony between Britain and America was not restored for several reasons. For one thing, on June 17, 1775, the Americans and the British fought the tremendous Battle of Bunker Hill, near Boston. Because they won the hill they wanted, the British technically won this battle, but they lost a thousand men in the process compared to

British and Hessian soldiers

400 American casualties. After this vicious battle, it was clear that a major war had begun. In addition, the king rejected the Olive Branch Petition and made plans to hire thousands of German soldiers, called *Hessians*, to fight the colonists.

The war in which America was freed from Britain is now called the American Revolution or the Revolutionary War. A revolution is a rather sudden, major change in a country's government brought about by armed conflict. Even after the Battle of Bunker Hill, most Americans were against a revolution. The prevailing thought was that the colonists had to fight Britain to gain more rights, but that America shouldn't separate from Britain. People referred to the war at the time as the American Rebellion.

Why weren't the colonists ready to cut the ties with Britain? Some Americans, mostly wealthy merchants who did business with Great Britain, feared that independence from the mother country would cost them their fortunes. Many of these people, the *Tories* or *Loyalists*, actually wanted Britain to squash the rebellion. Many Americans wanted their country to be free of Britain, but feared that America could not yet stand on its own. Many others were afraid that if America tried to break completely away from Britain and lost, the mother country would punish the colonies all the more.

Thomas Paine

A book helped convince Americans that they had to form a new country. Ironically, it was written by an Englishman: Thomas Paine.

At the urging of Ben Franklin, who was then in England presenting the American viewpoint, Paine had come to live in Philadelphia in late

1774. A strong booster of American independence, Paine in January of 1776 published a booklet called *Common Sense*, which offered basic arguments as to why America should separate from Great Britain.

First issue of Paine's *Common Sense*, 1776

Paine wrote that rule by kings and queens was a bad form of government because it prevented people from deciding basic issues for themselves. He argued that America gained nothing from its tie with Britain, but suffered in many ways because of it. He thought that it was silly for an island to rule a continent, and warned that since America was destined to be free of Britain, putting off independence would just leave the struggle for future generations. He added that America could be "the glory of the earth," and the best hope for oppressed people everywhere.

Common Sense became a best-seller, as several hundred thousand copies were sold in three months. Friends and neighbors discussed it with each other. Teachers read it to their classes. Those who couldn't read listened as ministers and public speakers read it to them. Thousands of people who had been hesitant about declaring independence were convinced by *Common Sense* that this was the best thing to do.

By spring of 1776, the independence movement was gaining steam. In April, North Carolina told its delegates at the Second Continental Congress to vote for independence. In May, Virginia told its delegates to propose independence.

The big step was taken by Richard Henry Lee of Virginia, who on June 7 introduced a stunning resolution to the Continental Congress. It said that "these United Colonies are, and of right ought to be free and independent states, that they are absolved from all allegiance to the British crown, and that all political connection between them and the state of Great Britain is, and ought to be totally dissolved." If Congress approved this resolution, it meant that the colonies were declaring their independence from Great Britain.

Richard Henry Lee

The delegates could not agree on what to do. Some favored independence, while others opposed it. Congress decided to put off a vote on the proposal until early July. But in case the vote came out in favor of independence, Congress wanted to have a paper ready explaining to the world why it had chosen that course. A committee of five men was assigned to produce a declaration of independence. The five were John Adams of Massachusetts, Ben Franklin of Pennsylvania,

Congressional committee drafting the Declaration of Independence

Robert R. Livingston of New York, Roger Sherman of Connecticut, and Thomas Jefferson of Virginia. The committee then assigned the job of writing the declaration to Thomas Jefferson.

Jefferson wrote the most famous document in American history, the Declaration of Independence, in late June of 1776. He did the writing at his desk in his Philadelphia apartment at Market and Seventh streets. Jefferson showed the

Declaration to Ben Franklin and John Adams. After they made a few changes, Jefferson turned the Declaration in to Congress.

Before approving the Declaration, Congress had to decide the independence issue. On July first and second, 1776, the State House on Philadelphia's Chestnut Street was the scene of the most crucial debate in the country's history. At times the discussions became quite heated. After a New York delegate said, "We're not ripe for independence," John Witherspoon of New Jersey shouted: "We're more than ripe for it! We are in danger of rotting for the lack of it!"

On July first—the day before the official vote— nine colonies favored independence. South Carolina and Pennsylvania opposed it. New York's delegates had been told not to vote on the question. Two of Delaware's delegates were split on the issue, and the third wasn't there yet. Although nine out of the thirteen was a majority, Congress knew that a decision for independence had to be backed by *all* the colonies. If two or three of them remained loyal to Britain, the colonies could end up fighting each other.

Before the big vote, those favoring independence pressured those who opposed it or were undecided. Then, late on July 2, Congress made the historic vote. The nine colonies which had favored independence on July 1 still favored it. Two of Pennsylvania's delegates who opposed independence—John Dickinson and Robert Morris—had decided not to vote on the issue. As a result, Pennsylvania squeaked by in favor of independence by a 3–2 vote. For the sake of going along with the majority, South Carolina also voted "Yes." And the third Delaware delegate, Caesar Rodney, completed an eighty-mile horseback ride to Philadelphia just in time to swing Delaware's vote to the independence side.

The final tally on July 2 showed New Hampshire, Massachusetts, Rhode Island, Connecticut, New Jersey, Pennsylvania, Delaware, Maryland, Virginia, North Carolina, South Carolina, and Georgia all for independence. The thirteenth colony, New York, did not vote that day, but made the vote unanimous a few days later.

The men of the Continental Congress thought that July 2, 1776, would be remembered as the birth date of the United States because that was the day they had voted for independence. Congress then turned its attention to the Declaration that was now needed. After making a few more changes in it, Congress adopted the

Declaration of Independence on July 4, 1776. Because the top of the Declaration said IN CONGRESS, JULY 4, 1776, Americans began celebrating July 4 instead of July 2 as the nation's birthday, and the practice has continued for over two centuries.

Copies of the Declaration were sent to towns throughout the thirteen "states," as they now called themselves. The Declaration was printed in newspapers and read to eager crowds. George Washington, appointed commander in chief of American forces by Congress in 1775, had the Declaration read to his army. In Philadelphia, the Declaration was read to a crowd in the State House yard, and the bell (later called the Liberty Bell) in the State House tower was rung.

The Declaration was signed by most members of the Continental Congress in early August of 1776. Several men who had been against independence earlier signed the document anyway, either because they had changed their minds or to show unanimity. Nine men signed the Declaration for Pennsylvania—more than from any other state. The nine were Robert Morris, Benjamin Rush, Benjamin Franklin, John Morton, George Clymer, James Smith, George Taylor, James Wilson, and George Ross.

At Congress's urging, the new states organized new state governments. Pennsylvania very quickly adopted a new state constitution that was one of the most democratic frames of government of the time. The new state government first met in Philadelphia in late November of 1776, while the national Congress was also still meeting in the city.

Independence had been declared with the pen, but it had to be won on the battlefield. On the day that the Declaration was read to his troops, George Washington told them that the future of the country depended "solely on the success of our arms," meaning success in battle. For several years it appeared that the United States would not have success in arms and that the states would become colonies once again. The men in Washington's army were poorly fed, poorly clothed, poorly paid, poorly trained, and they lacked guns and ammunition.* Some of them disliked following orders, and answered "Do it yourself!" when officers gave them commands. When it was time to plant or harvest crops, soldiers deserted the army by the thousands. Many hundreds even went over to the British side.

To make things worse, America had few good

General George
Washington

* For more information about the army see page 153

military leaders besides Washington. Several top-ranking men were so jealous of Washington that they tried to have him removed as commander in chief, and several were so hungry for glory that they came up with foolish schemes that wasted lives and time. The American army was so disorganized that soldiers sometimes fired on each other instead of on the enemy.

In Pennsylvania, little went right for the Americans. During September of 1777, British troops invaded the state. Washington tried to stop them from entering Philadelphia by fighting them at Brandywine Creek, about twenty-five miles southwest of Philadelphia on September 11. But Washington's 10,000-man army was no match for General William Howe's 15,000 soldiers. The British won the Battle of Brandywine, suffering 600 casualties compared to 1,000 for the patriots. On September 26, the British moved into Philadelphia.

Wherever the Continental Congress was meeting was considered the United States capital. Just before the British entered Philadelphia, Congress packed up and moved out. Congress met in Lancaster, Pennsylvania for one day—September 27, 1777. Moving around like an orphan, Congress met for a few months in York,

General William Howe

127

Pennsylvania, a short while later. Lancaster and York both have the honor of having served as United States capitals.

Meanwhile, General Washington very much wanted to win Philadelphia back from the redcoats. On October 4, 1777, Washington sent 11,000 patriot soldiers against about 9,000 British troops at Germantown (now part of Philadelphia). The attack failed, partly because in the fog two American units mistook each other for the British and fired on one another. The Americans lost about 650 men in the Battle of Germantown, while the victorious British lost about 550.

The Battle of Germantown

Washington decided that he and his troops would make their winter quarters at Valley Forge, Pennsylvania, about twenty-five miles west of Philadelphia. Flanked by the Schuylkill River and high ground, this level plateau seemed rather safe from enemy attack. But if the British did attack, Washington and his troops could escape into the wilds of western Pennsylvania. Also, if the chance to strike the British near Philadelphia presented itself, that was also possible from Valley Forge.

On December 19, 1777, Washington led his 11,000 ragged men into Valley Forge. Half the men did not have shoes, and as they marched over the frozen ground their bleeding feet left a red trail. The morning after their arrival, Washington divided his troops into twelve-man units. Each unit was to build a hut sixteen feet long, fourteen feet wide, and six and a half feet high. Washington offered a twelve-dollar prize to the unit that finished its hut first. The winners finished within a couple of days, and by early January hundreds of huts had been built.

The men suffered terribly during that winter at Valley Forge. The huts didn't completely protect them from the bitter cold, and there was a shortage of clothes and blankets. On some days, the men had nothing to eat, and at other times all

The bitter-cold winter at Valley Forge

they had were "fire cakes"—moist flour grilled over hot embers. Disease also set in. Martha Washington (George Washington's wife) tended the sick along with many of the other wives and girlfriends who wintered with their men at Valley Forge. But they couldn't prevent the deaths of more than 3,000 of the soldiers during that winter of 1777–1778.

The conditions at Valley Forge became so bad that even those loyal followers of George Washington were on the verge of mutiny. Washington begged Congress to send the men food and clothes, but Congress couldn't afford to help. It was largely due to Washington's efforts that the army kept from disbanding during that awful winter.*

Baron Friedrich von Steuben

A German soldier, Baron Friedrich von Steuben, also helped lift the men's spirits at Valley Forge. On Ben Franklin's suggestion, George Washington had hired von Steuben to teach the soldiers to march and drill. By springtime, the survivors of Valley Forge still looked ragged, but they knew how to march and load their guns like professional soldiers.

The spring brought very good news. Due mainly to Ben Franklin's efforts, in February of 1778 France joined the war on the American side.

* For more information about Valley Forge see page 153

France was the second-most powerful country in the world and had nearly defeated Britain in the French and Indian War. Perhaps Britain would have beaten the Americans alone in the war, but it could not beat the combined efforts of the Americans *and* the French.

Between 1778 and 1780, the Americans did well in several battles and forced the British to give up some of the territory they had already won. The British left Philadelphia in June of 1778, so the city once again became the United States capital. The final major battle of the war was fought at Yorktown, Virginia, in fall of 1781. After losing the Battle of Yorktown to the American and French forces, British General Cornwallis had to surrender to George Washington. This great American victory meant that the United States had won the war!

General Charles Earl Cornwallis

Benjamin Franklin helped negotiate the peace treaty that was made between the United States and Great Britain in 1783. Once the peace treaty was signed on September 3 of that year, it meant that even the British recognized that a new country, the United States of America, had been born!

JOHN DICKINSON (1732–1808)

John Dickinson

John Dickinson was born in Maryland but moved with his family to Delaware when he was eight years old. John's father had taken a homeless young Irish tutor named William Killen into the Dickinson family. Although only ten years older than John, Killen taught the boy literature, essay writing, Latin, and other languages. With Killen's help, by age eighteen John was one of the best-educated young people in the colonies.

In preparation for a law career, John Dickinson went to work for a noted Philadelphia lawyer, and later went to London to study law. He returned to Philadelphia in 1757 to begin his own law career and soon was one of the best-known lawyers in Pennsylvania. John Dickinson found that he was more interested in politics than in practicing law, though. He was elected to the Assembly of Delaware, which was then still part of Pennsylvania, in fall of 1760. Two years later, Philadelphians elected him to the Pennsylvania Assembly.

John Dickinson was one of the leading opponents of the Stamp Act. In 1767–1768, he published a series of letters describing British injustices in the *Pennsylvania Chronicle*. These famous *Letters from a Farmer in Pennsylvania* were read or listened to by people in all thirteen colonies.

Dickinson was a delegate from Pennsylvania to both the First and Second Continental Congresses. While in Congress, he earned the nickname the "Penman of the Revolution." In 1775, he wrote Congress's "Declaration announcing to the world our reasons at taking up arms against England." Yet, because he thought that the colonists were not ready for independence, and because he was a Quaker and hated war, Dickinson opposed the Declaration of Independence and did not show up when Congress voted on it.

Dickinson was a mystery to people of his own and later times. Why did he write the declaration for taking up arms if he opposed independence? And why didn't he vote against independence if that was his opinion?

The answer was that Dickinson considered the majority opinion "sacred." As one of the country's best writers, he was willing to express Congress's general opinion even when it differed from his own. And, seeing that most Congressmen favored independence by July of 1776, he did not want to oppose what he later called "the voice of my country."

John Dickinson then did something that puzzled people all the more. He became one of only several Congressmen to actually fight as a soldier during the war, serving at the Battle of Brandywine and at other places. Although he was a man of peace, he chose to defend his country once there was no chance for a peaceful solution.

In 1781, John Dickinson was elected governor of Delaware. Then, returning to live in Philadelphia, he was elected and served as governor of Pennsylvania from 1782 to 1785. He went to the Constitutional Convention in 1787 as a delegate from Delaware. At the convention, he helped create the system by which each state has two senators, but a number of representatives in the House that is based on population.

This man of peace helped found Dickinson College in Carlisle, Pennsylvania, which is named for him. He also worked to end slavery, educate poor children, and improve conditions in prisons. The "Penman of the Revolution" died at the age of 75 in Wilmington, Delaware.

ROBERT MORRIS (1734–1806)

Robert Morris

Robert Morris was born and spent his childhood in Liverpool, England. When Robert was about four years old, his father sailed to Maryland where he represented an English company. About nine years later, Mr. Morris sent for his thirteen-year-old son. Robert stayed with his father for only about a year, apparently because the two of them did not get along. In 1748, Robert went to live in Philadelphia, where he briefly attended school and was soon apprenticed to prominent merchant Charles Willing.

When Robert was sixteen, his father died, leaving him on his own in the new world. Robert not only survived, he soon earned a reputation as a financial wizard. Once when Mr. Willing was out of the country, Robert heard that the price of flour was about to rise sharply. Robert rushed out and bought all the flour he could find. When the price of flour rose the next day, he made a lot of money for the Willing company. Robert was so good at determining what goods to buy and when to buy and sell them that he was made a partner in the Willing firm while still in his early twenties. He went to Jamaica several times to sell goods for the firm. The French and Indian War was then raging, and on one trip Robert's ship was captured by French privateers near Cuba. After a number of adventures, he made his way back to Philadelphia several months later.

By the age of thirty, Robert Morris was one of Philadelphia's leading merchants. He was also becoming one of the country's leading patriots. Morris strongly opposed the Stamp Act of 1765, and a decade later Pennsylvania sent him to the Second Continental Congress. Although he sought fairer treatment for America, by summer of 1776 Morris still did not think the colonies were ready for independence. Robert Morris and John Dickinson did not want to prevent Pennsylvania from siding with the other colonies, though, which was why they stayed home for the July 2 vote on independence. Once the choice was made, Robert Morris devoted himself to the independence cause, and he signed the Declaration with the other delegates later in the summer.

During the Revolutionary War, Congress assigned Robert Morris the job of obtaining money to pay for soldiers and supplies. Morris convinced merchants and friends to loan money to the United States. Often he took personal responsibility for the loans, meaning that if the United States couldn't repay the money he would have to pay it back himself. He also personally provided the army with lead for bullets and large amounts of flour for bread.

Just before the Battle of Yorktown, some of George Washington's soldiers threatened to quit unless they were given at least a month's worth of their back pay. Morris borrowed the money from the French, from his friends, and from his fellow merchants. The soldiers continued on to Yorktown, where they won a crucial battle against the British.

Between 1781 and 1784, Robert Morris served as Superintendent of Finance of the United States. One of his first acts was to create the Bank of North America in Philadelphia—the country's first successful bank.

Robert Morris attended the Constitutional Convention in 1787. Although he didn't say much at the convention, it is thought that his talkative friend Gouverneur Morris (no relation to Robert) expressed the views of both of them. Robert Morris was one of the Pennsylvania signers of the Constitution, and two years later he was elected one of Pennsylvania's first two United States senators, serving for six years until 1795.

Robert Morris' personal goal was to become the richest person in America. Unfortunately, the "Financier of the Revolution" made a number of bad investments late in life. Not only did he lose his money, he ended up owing a great deal. He sank so low that he even spent three and a half years in debtors' prison in Philadelphia and died in poverty at the age of seventy-two. The town of Morrisville, Pennsylvania, along the Delaware River northeast of Philadelphia, is named for him.

Haym Salomon

HAYM SALOMON (1740?–1785)

Haym Salomon was born in what is now Poland in about 1740. He spent his early years traveling through Europe, where he learned a great deal about finance, languages, and people. After returning to Poland aboout 1770, he worked for that country's independence. But in 1772—

the year that Austria, Prussia, and Russia seized much of Poland—Salomon left his native land and came to New York City, where he opened a brokerage house and a dry-goods business. Salomon was very skilled at buying goods that came in on ships and selling them at a profit.

Conditions in Salomon's new country resembled those in Poland in an important way. Americans were also seeking liberty. Haym Salomon was one of several thousand Jews who lived in America during the revolutionary era. The Jewish Americans overwhelmingly favored independence, and a relatively large percentage of their people joined George Washington's army. Haym Salomon was no soldier, but he helped in his own way.

At the start of the war, Salomon helped supply provisions for the American soldiers in upper New York State. Soon after the British seized New York City in September of 1776, they arrested Salomon as an American spy. The British couldn't prove him guilty, though, and they also had another reason to release him. Since Salomon knew German, the British made him serve as translator for the Hessian soldiers who were fighting on their side.

Salomon didn't just translate the orders the British officers gave the Hessians. He also whispered advice in the Germans' ears. "Leave the British army and join our side," he told them. "We will give you land if you do." In summer of 1778, the British again arrested Salomon as a spy. They also accused him of sheltering escaped American prisoners in his home, and of working with patriots who had planned to burn British ships in New York Harbor. This time Salomon was sentenced to die.

One night in August of 1778, Haym Salomon was spending what seemed to be his last few hours. He was scheduled to hang at dawn, and there was an armed guard outside his locked cell. But Salomon began telling the guard to open the cell door, run away, and join the American side. Salomon then offered the guard some gold coins he had somehow managed to hide. The guard took the bribe. Soon Haym Salomon was out of jail and running for his life.

Word of his escape spread, and Salomon had many close calls with capture as he headed to Philadelphia, which was then under patriot control. Salomon had left his wife and child in New York City, but he couldn't go back for them because the British were on the lookout for him there.

Soon after entering Philadelphia as a pauper, Salomon went down to the waterfront and watched the ships being unloaded. Finally he spotted a bargain. He bought the merchandise, promising to pay the merchant by the next day. Salomon immediately sold the goods to another merchant for a higher price, in cash. After paying the first merchant, he still had a profit for himself. Salomon had again gone to work as a broker—someone who buys goods or lands and sells them at a profit.

Salomon's knowledge of finance and languages enabled him to deal with merchants from many different countries. He earned a fortune operating his Philadelphia brokerage firm, but kept little of the money for himself. Salomon knew that the United States could not win the war against Britain unless it had money to pay its soldiers and run its government, and he helped provide some of those desperately-needed funds.

Salomon put up about half a million dollars to help the revolutionary cause. He paid the salaries of government workers and soldiers. He paid other government debts, and helped secure loans from France. When Robert Morris, the American Superintendent of Finance, needed money for the American cause, Haym Salomon helped him again and again.

Not long after arriving in Philadelphia, Haym Salomon had arranged for his wife and child to come there from New York. But Salomon didn't get to enjoy his family for very long. Salomon's health had broken down while he had been in the British jail, and he died at about age forty-five soon after the Revolutionary War ended. Haym Salomon left his family nearly penniless at his death, but he had helped his adopted country gain its liberty.

BETSY ROSS (1752–1836)

The eighth of seventeen children, Betsy Griscom was born in Philadelphia on New Year's Day, 1752. Betsy's father was a Quaker and she is thought to have attended a Quaker school on Fourth Street.

When Betsy was twenty-one, she married John Ross, nephew of George Ross, a Pennsylvania signer of the Declaration of Independence. Knowing that her friends and family would oppose the marriage because John was not a Quaker, Betsy eloped with John to New Jersey.

After the newlyweds returned to Philadelphia, John Ross opened a shop where he upholstered furniture. But in early 1776, John was killed by a gunpowder explosion on a wharf that he was guarding. Betsy Ross, as she was now known, continued to operate the upholstery shop and earned a reputation around Philadelphia as an excellent seamstress.

Because they did not want the British to know what they were doing, the American patriots were very secretive, and so many details about Revolutionary War events are unknown. One of the questions that has never been answered for certain is: Who made the first United States flag with stars and stripes on it? Many people think that it was Betsy Ross.

Betsy Ross

According to a famous story, in June of 1776 George Washington, Robert Morris, and George Ross visited Betsy Ross. The three men asked her to make a flag for the new country, and gave her a rough idea of the kind they had in mind. Betsy was said to have made at least one change in their plan. She thought that the flag's thirteen stars (representing the thirteen states) should be five-sided, instead of six-sided as the men proposed. Then, according to tradition, Betsy Ross made the first Stars and Stripes.

Papers have been found which prove that Betsy Ross *did* make a number of flags for the new United States. But whether she made the very *first* American flag with stars and stripes cannot be proven. The other main contender for this honor is Francis Hopkinson, a Philadelphia-born man who practiced law in New Jersey and Pennsylvania and who signed the Declaration of Independence from New Jersey.

As for Betsy Ross, she continued working as a seamstress until the age of seventy-five, when she turned the business over to a daughter. She outlived a total of three husbands, and died in Philadelphia at the age of eighty-four.

The Signing of the Constitution, 1787

Chapter IX

The Second State

We the people of the United States, in order to form a more perfect Union, establish justice, insure domestic tranquility, provide for the common defense, promote the general welfare, and secure the blessings of liberty to ourselves and our posterity, do ordain and establish this Constitution for the United States of America.

Beginning of the United States Constitution, created in Philadelphia in 1787

During the United States' first years, it appeared that the country would not be able to stand on its own, just as some people had feared. The new country was governed by the Articles of Confederation, a set of national laws that had been approved by the thirteen states in 1781. But the Articles granted so little power to the central government (the Continental Congress) that the government was almost useless.

In most ways, each state was more powerful than the national government. The individual states could raise more money and form a bigger army than could the national government. Most

Americans in the years 1781–85 wanted things to be like that. Although people across the country had worked together to free themselves from Britain, most people felt more loyalty to their individual states than to the nation as a whole. People also worried that a strong central government would tax them a great deal and control their lives too much.

There was a long list of ways in which the federal government was almost helpless. The entire U.S. Army consisted of only several hundred men. The nation had no president to lead it, and no federal courts. Because the country had no national currency, each state had to print its own money.

The federal government also lacked the power to collect taxes. When it needed money, Congress had to beg the states for it. Most of the states ignored these requests. In a typical year, Congress might ask for about $8,000,000 and get only $400,000. As a result, the Congress could not pay its debts. In summer of 1783, about a hundred soldiers who were owed money by the federal government marched on the State House in Phila-delphia, where Congress was meeting. The soldiers demanded their back pay, but Congress didn't have it. Congress then packed up, left Phila-delphia, and ran away to Princeton, New Jersey, which then became the nation's new capital!

Given this sad state of affairs, the country's best lawmakers preferred to work in state government. Many of the men in the Congress were what we might call "second-stringers." Gouverneur Morris of Pennsylvania once referred to them as "a lot of rascals."

Because the United States did not always honor its promises to them, foreign countries did not take the U.S. government seriously. Great Britain and Spain both refused to honor agreements it had made with the United States. There was even the danger that, due to the weakness of its central government, the United States would be conquered by a foreign power.

Finally, in many cases, the states did not get along with each other. New York argued with New Jersey and Connecticut over financial matters. Maryland and Virginia feuded, too. The U.S. government couldn't settle these disputes between the states any more than a first grader could settle a fight between two eighth graders. There were so many arguments between the states that George Washington said, "I see one

A government supporter
fights a Shay supporter
during Shay's Rebellion.

head gradually changing into thirteen."

Several key events made people realize that the country needed a stronger national government. One was Shays' Rebellion, a revolt by western Massachusetts farmers that lasted from fall of 1786 until early 1787. In this rebellion, Daniel Shays and his followers demanded lower taxes and an end to the imprisonment of people who owed large sums of money. The Massachusetts militia had to squash this revolt because the federal government lacked the army to handle the problem.

By 1787, a large segment of the American population wanted a stronger national government. To reorganize the government, a national convention met in Philadelphia from May to September of 1787. The delegates met in the Pennsylvania State House, the very building where the Declaration of Independence had been created.

Seven dollars in Continental Currency

At first many of the delegates planned to merely improve the Articles of Confederation. But in order to amend the Articles, all thirteen states had to approve the changes. There was little chance that all thirteen states could agree on *anything!* Besides that, Rhode Island had not even sent any delegates to the convention because it feared being swallowed up by a more powerful central government. The men at the convention decided to produce a new set of national laws, which we call the United States Constitution.

Several of the Pennsylvania delegates were among the leaders in creating the new Constitution. Pennsylvania's Gouverneur Morris made impassioned speeches against slavery, but the

Southern delegates would not permit the Constitution to ban slavery. Morris also headed the committee that wrote the Constitution's final draft. Pennsylvania's James Wilson was one of the main promoters of a strong central government. Wilson said that the "whole" (the federal government) should no longer be "at the mercy of the parts" (the states). He also said that the federal government should derive its authority from the people, not from the states. Pennsylvania's Ben Franklin, the oldest delegate, contributed by telling a funny story or by finding another way to keep peace at times when the arguing got out of control.

The inkstand used during the Constitutional Convention

The Constitution was completed by September of 1787. As with the Declaration of Independence, Pennsylvania had the most signers of the Constitution. The eight signers of the Constitution for Pennsylvania were Benjamin Franklin, Thomas Mifflin, Robert Morris, George Clymer, Thomas FitzSimons, Jared Ingersoll, James Wilson, and Gouverneur Morris.

Each of the ex-colonies would become a state under the new Constitution on the day that it ratified (approved) the Constitution. And the Constitution would become the law of the whole

WE the People of the States of New-Hampfhire, Maffachufetts, Rhode-Ifland and Providence Plantations, Connecticut, New-York, New-Jerfey, Pennfylvania, Delaware, Maryland, Virginia, North-Carolina, South-Carolina, and Georgia, do ordain, declare and eftablifh the following Conftitution for the Government of Ourfelves and our Pofterity.

ARTICLE I.

The ftile of this Government fhall be, " The United States of America."

II.

The Government fhall confift of fupreme legiflative, executive and judicial powers.

III.

The legiflative power lhall be vefted in a Congrefs, to confift of two feparate and diftinct bodies of men, a Houfe of Reprefentatives, and a Senate; ~~each of which fhall, in all cafes, have a negative on the other. The Legiflature fhall meet on the firft Monday in December in every year.~~

*The Legiflature fhall meet at leaft once in every year: and that meeting fhall be on the firft Monday in December unlefs a different day fhall be appointed by law.

IV.

A draft of the Constitution

country when it had been approved by nine of the thirteen states.

Delaware, which had once been part of Pennsylvania, became the first state when it ratified the Constitution on December 7, 1787. Pennsylvania, where the Declaration of Independence and the U.S. Constitution had been written, and where the army had survived the horrors of Valley Forge, became the second state by ratifying the Constitution five days later, on December 12.

The Constitution went into effect when New Hampshire, the ninth state, ratified it in June of 1788. And on May 29, 1790, Rhode Island became the thirteenth state by ratifying the great document that had been created in Philadelphia three years earlier.

JAMES WILSON (1742-1798)

James Wilson

James Wilson was born in Scotland, where his family lived on a farm. He began a university education with the idea of becoming a minister, but his father's death forced him to leave school. James worked for a while as a tutor, but soon decided that America was the place where he could make his mark. He arrived in New York in 1765, and by the next year he had gone to live in Philadelphia where he taught Latin in the college that later became the University of Pennsylvania.

An outstanding speaker and writer, James Wilson decided that he wanted to be a lawyer. After working for about a year in John Dickinson's law office, he became a lawyer himself in 1767. In 1770, he settled in Carlisle, Pennsylvania, about a hundred miles west of Philadelphia. A year later, he married, and within a short time he was considered one of the best lawyers in the colony.

The young man from Scotland had come to America at the start of the troubles with Britain. Wilson sided strongly with his adopted country and was one of the first people in America to conclude that Parliament had no authority over the colonies. However, as a Pennsylvania delegate to the Continental Congress, Wilson at first sided with John Dickinson in opposing complete independence. Almost at the last moment, he decided to vote for independence on July 2, 1776, enabling Pennsylvania to support independence by a 3-2 vote.

James Wilson made his greatest contribution to his country at the Constitutional Convention in 1787, however. Another Pennsylvanian, Gouverneur Morris, spoke the most at the Convention, but Wilson spoke the second-most. He was one of the most democratic of all the delegates. Again and again, he said that the people were the foundation for the government, that the government was there to serve the people, and that the people should elect their lawmakers directly.

After signing the Constitution, James Wilson worked to get it approved by Pennsylvania. In a thrilling speech he made in the State House yard in fall of 1787, Wilson said that although he didn't agree with every detail, the Constitution was as good a plan as a group of people could create. He even called the Constitution "the best form of government which has ever been offered to the world." Wilson played a central role at the ratifying convention in Philadelphia which approved the Constitution on December 12, 1787.

In 1789, George Washington appointed James Wilson to be one of the first associate justices of the United States Supreme Court. He served as an associate justice for the rest of his life. Unfortunately, like Robert Morris, James Wilson made bad business deals and ended up poor. To avoid arrest for debt, he fled to New Jersey and then North Carolina. One of James Wilson's last written comments was that he had been hunted "like a wild beast" by people who wanted to collect money from him. James Wilson died at the age of fifty-five in North Carolina.

GOUVERNEUR MORRIS (1752–1816)

Gouverneur Morris

Gouverneur Morris was born on his family's large estate, Morrisania, in what is now New York City. His first name, which had been his mother's maiden name, confused people, especially once he reached adulthood. Some people thought he was governor of a state when they were introduced to "Gouverneur Morris." Had he become a governor things would have really been confusing, for then he would have been Governor Gouverneur Morris. Morris was a very handsome, athletic, and intelligent child. By age ten, he was studying Latin, Greek, geography, history, and writing at the academy Ben Franklin had helped found in Philadelphia. He was also a fun-loving person and a prankster all his life. One day Morris and his schoolmates closed the shutters of the classroom and then locked their Latin teacher inside with them. The students yelled and threw Latin books at the teacher, who had to hide under a desk in the darkened toom. The students did this to the poor man several times, until school officials found out about it and made them stop.

At just twelve years of age, Morris was admitted to King's College (now Columbia University) in New York City. He graduated from King's College at sixteen, then went to work as a law clerk with a New York City lawyer. There were no xerox machines in those days, so much of Morris' work consisted of copying documents over and over. But he learned enough law from his employer to become a lawyer himself at the age of nineteen.

When Gouverneur Morris reached his early twenties, the troubles with Britain began. At first, he opposed American independence, but by 1776 he favored it. In 1778 and 1779, he served in the Continental Congress as a New York delegate. Because of his superb writing ability, he drafted a number of important papers for Congress. He also spent some time at Valley Forge talking to George Washington about plans to reorganize the army. Morris became good friends with Washington, and was considered his strongest supporter in Congress.

Near the end of the Revolutionary War, Gouverneur Morris moved to Philadelphia. Shortly after this move, his left leg was badly injured in a fall from his carriage. The leg was amputated and he was fitted with a wooden peg. When friends said that he looked fine without his leg, Morris

147

jokingly answered that perhaps he should have the other one removed in order to look even better.

From 1781 to 1785, Morris served as the country's Assistant Superintendent of Finance under his good friend Robert Morris. Then on the next to the last day of 1786, the Pennsylvania General Assembly elected Gouverneur Morris as a delegate to the Constitutional Convention.

Morris made more speeches—nearly 200—than any other delegate to the Constitutional Convention. He spoke in favor of a very strong central government and against slavery. Gouverneur Morris also wrote much of the final draft of the Constitution. The ideas in the Constitution came from the entire Convention, but much of the wording was Morris's.

One amusing story about Gouverneur Morris concerns a bet he made with Alexander Hamilton of New York. Just as people today are in awe of George Washington, so were people back in Washington's time. People stared at Washington wherever he went, and no one joked around with him. Gouverneur Morris bet Alexander Hamilton that he could act like a buddy to Washington. The three of them were at a large dinner party when Morris suddenly slapped Washington on the back and said, "Wasn't it so, my old boy?" Everyone at the party thought that Morris had lost his mind. He won the bet, but because Washington was a little annoyed with him, Morris told Hamilton that he was sorry for what he'd done.

Between 1792 and 1794, Gouverneur Morris served as United States minister to France, and between 1800 and 1803 he was a United States senator from New York. The man who had penned most of the final draft of the Constitution died at Morrisania at the age of sixty-four.

James Claypoole
ffrancis Plumsted
Thomas Barker
Philip fford
Edward Prichard
Andrew Sowle

Christopher Taylor
Charles floyd
William Gibson
Richard Davies
N. More
Geo Rudyard
Harbt Springett

William Penn's signature and seal to the Pennsylvania Charter; thirteen witnesses also signed (above). Receipt from 1682 for money given to the Committee of the Free Society of Traders in Pennsylvania (below).

London The Eight and Twentith day of the 7 th Month, called September 1682 Received in then of Hannah Anderdon of Bridgwater Spinster the Summ of Twelve pounds Ten Shillings Sterling, for the use of the Free Society of Traders in Pennsilvania, Witness Our hands and the Societys Seal

N More } President
James Claypoole } Treasurer

N° 184

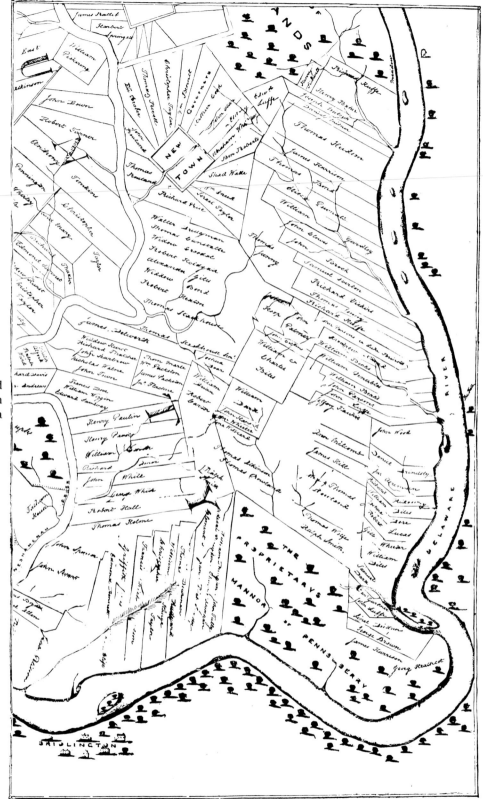

1683 map shows land ownership in Pennsylvania

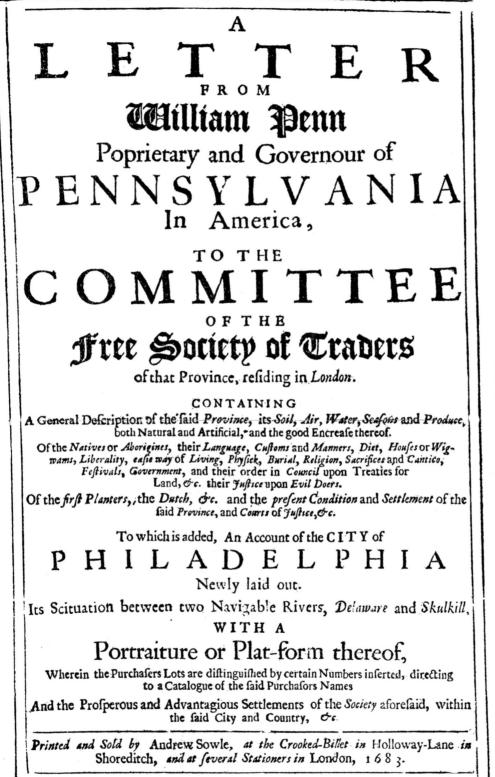

A LETTER

FROM

William Penn

Poprietary and Governour of

PENNSYLVANIA

In America,

TO THE

COMMITTEE

OF THE

Free Society of Traders

of that Province, residing in London.

CONTAINING

A General Description of the said *Province*, its *Soil, Air, Water, Seasons* and *Produce*, both Natural and Artificial, and the good Encrease thereof.

Of the *Natives* or *Aborigines*, their *Language, Customs* and *Manners, Diet, Houses* or *Wigwams, Liberality, easie way* of *Living, Physick, Burial, Religion, Sacrifices* and *Cantico, Festivals, Government*, and their order in *Council* upon Treaties for Land, &c. their *Justice* upon *Evil Doers*.

Of the *first Planters*, the *Dutch, &c.* and the *present Condition* and *Settlement* of the said *Province*, and *Courts* of *Justice, &c.*

To which is added, An Account of the CITY of

PHILADELPHIA

Newly laid out.

Its Scituation between two Navigable Rivers, *Delaware* and *Skulkill*,

WITH A

Portraiture or Plat-form thereof,

Wherein the Purchasers Lots are distinguished by certain Numbers inserted, directing to a Catalogue of the said Purchasors Names

And the Prosperous and Advantagious Settlements of the *Society* aforesaid, within the said City and Country, &c.

Printed and Sold by Andrew Sowle, *at the Crooked-Billet in* Holloway-Lane *in* Shoreditch, *and at several Stationers in* London, 1 6 8 3.

Letter from William Penn to the Committee of the Free Society of Traders

Received from the honorable Thomas and Richard
Penn Esq'rs true and absolute Proprietaries of Pennsyl.
vania by the hands of the honorable Sir William Johnson
Baronet the Sum of ten thousand Dollars being the
full consideration of the Lands lately sold to them by
the Indians of the six Nations at the late Treaty of
Fort Stanwix We say received this Twenty Eighth
day of July — Anno Domini 1769 — for ourselves
and the other Indians of the six Nations and their confederacy
and dependant Tribes for whom we act and by whom
we are appointed and empowered —

A Receipt from the
Six Nations for
£10000 Currency or
10000 Dollars.

Wittness present
Henry Tray Luotig
Jacob Cook Clark Justice
Nor. MacLeod
Pat Daly

Abraham, for the Mohawks

Johannes Tekariho

Jonathan Kayeagus

Joseph Thayendase

James Suharovane

Lodowick Aughnainte

Joseph Tagahesaron

Tayuni

Anahgogare

Onoghranoron

Onughshiony

For the Cayuga Nation
by the desire of the whole

Amaqualecka

Serrehounas

Treaty with Indian tribes, 1769.

In ASSEMBLY, December 12, 1776.

WHEREAS there is a Neceffity of calling upon the ASSOCIATORS of Penn-fylvania, at this inclement Seafon, to affift in defending their Country threatened with inftant Invafion,

Refolved, That over and above all Encouragement heretofore offered, the following Bounties be given to all Volunteers who fhall join General WASHINGTON by the feveral Days hereunder mentioned:

On or before the 20th of this Month — 10 Dollars.
Between the 20th and 25th ——— 7 Dollars.
Between the 25th and 30th ——— 5 Dollars.

The Volunteers to be well armed, and with each of them a Blanket, and to remain in the fervice fix Weeks, unlefs fooner difcharged; the Bounty to be paid immediately on their Arrival at Camp; and, that no Time may be loft, the Volunteers are exhorted not to wait at home to be collected into Companies, but that they march off with the utmoft Speed, to be formed on their Arrival.

But it is not meant or intended to difcourage the Affociators from coming, with their Officers, in Battalions or Companies, in the Whole, or in Part, which will be moft agreeable,

Refolved, That the firft mentioned Bounty of ten Dollars be extended to the Inhabitants of the City and Liberties of Philadelphia not poffeffed of real Eftates, and to all other Volunteers, without Limitation of Property, who have already joined General Wafhington, and fhall ferve the above Time.

Extracts from the Minutes.

JOSIAH CRAWFORD, Clerk Pro. Tem.

Pay scale for men willing to fight in the army (above). Washington's plea to Pennsylvania farmers to send supplies to Valley Forge (below).

By His EXCELLENCY

GEORGE WASHINGTON, Esquire,

GENERAL and COMMANDER in CHIEF of the Forces of the UNITED STATES OF AMERICA.

BY Virtue of the Power and Direction, to Me efpecially given, I hereby enjoin and require all Perfons refiding within feventy Miles of my Head Quarters to threfh one Half of their Grain by the 1ft Day of February, and the other Half by the 1ft Day of March next enfuing, on Pain, in Cafe of Failure, of having all that fhall remain in Sheaves after the Period above mentioned, feized by the Commiffaries and Quarter-Mafters of the Army, and paid for as Straw.

GIVEN under my Hand, at Head Quarters, near the Valley Forge, in Philadelphia County, this 20th Day of December, 1777.

G. WASHINGTON.

By His Excellency's Command,

ROBERT H. HARRISON, Sec'y.

LANCASTER; Printed by JOHN DUNLAP.

Colonial America Time Line

Before the arrival of Europeans, many millions of Indians belonging to dozens of tribes lived in North America (and also in Central and South America)

About 982 A.D.—Eric the Red, born in Norway, reaches Greenland during one of the first European voyages to North America

About 985—Eric the Red brings settlers from Iceland to Greenland

About 1000—Leif Ericson (Eric the Red's son) leads what is thought to be the first European expedition to mainland North America; Leif probably lands in Canada

1492—Christopher Columbus, sailing for Spain, reaches America

1497—John Cabot reaches Canada in the first English voyage to North America

1513—Ponce de León of Spain explores Florida

1519-1521—Hernando Cortés of Spain conquers Mexico

1565—St. Augustine, Florida, the first permanent European town in what is now the United States, is founded by the Spanish

1607—Jamestown, Virginia is founded, the first permanent English town in the present-day U.S.

1608—Frenchman Samuel de Champlain founds the village of Quebec, Canada

1609—Henry Hudson explores the eastern coast of present-day U.S. for The Netherlands; the Dutch then claim parts of New York, New Jersey, Delaware, and Connecticut and name the area New Netherland

1619—Virginia's House of Burgesses, America's first representative lawmaking body, is founded

1619—The first shipment of black slaves arrives in Jamestown

1620—English Pilgrims found Massachusetts' first permanent town at Plymouth

1621—Massachusetts Pilgrims and Indians hold the famous first Thanksgiving feast in colonial America

1622—Indians kill 347 settlers in Virginia

1623—Colonization of New Hampshire is begun by the English

1624—Colonization of present-day New York State is begun by the Dutch at Fort Orange (Albany)

1625—The Dutch start building New Amsterdam (now New York City)

1630—The town of Boston, Massachusetts is founded by the English Puritans

1633—Colonization of Connecticut is begun by the English

1634—Colonization of Maryland is begun by the English

1635—Boston Latin School, the colonies' first public school, is founded

1636—Harvard, the colonies' first college, is founded in Massachusetts

1636—Rhode Island colonization begins when Englishman Roger Williams founds Providence

1638—The colonies' first library is established at Harvard

1638—Delaware colonization begins when Swedish people build Fort Christina at present-day Wilmington

1640—Stephen Daye of Cambridge, Massachusetts prints *The Bay Psalm Book*, the first English-language book published in what is now the U.S.

1643—Swedish settlers begin colonizing Pennsylvania

1647—Massachusetts forms the first public school system in the colonies

1650—North Carolina is colonized by Virginia settlers in about this year

1650—Population of colonial U.S. is about 50,000

1660—New Jersey colonization is begun by the Dutch at present-day Jersey City

1670—South Carolina colonization is begun by the English near Charleston

1673—Jacques Marquette and Louis Jolliet explore the upper Mississippi River for France

1675-76—New England colonists beat Indians in King Philip's War

1682—Philadelphia, Pennsylvania is settled

1682—La Salle explores Mississippi River all the way to its mouth in Louisiana and claims the whole Mississippi Valley for France

1693—College of William and Mary is founded in Williamsburg, Virginia

1700—Colonial population is about 250,000

1704—*The Boston News-Letter*, the first successful newspaper in the colonies, is founded

1706—Benjamin Franklin is born in Boston

1732—George Washington, future first president of the United States, is born in Virginia

1733—English begin colonizing Georgia, their thirteenth colony in what is now the United States

1735—John Adams, future second president, is born in Massachusetts

1743—Thomas Jefferson, future third president, is born in Virginia

1750—Colonial population is about 1,200,000

1754—France and England begin fighting the French and Indian War over North American lands

1763—England, victorious in the war, gains Canada and most other French lands east of the Mississippi River

1764—British pass Sugar Act to gain tax money from the colonists

1765—British pass the Stamp Act, which the colonists despise; colonists then hold the Stamp Act Congress in New York City

1766—British repeal the Stamp Act

1770—British soldiers kill five Americans in the "Boston Massacre"

1773—Colonists dump British tea into Boston Harbor at the "Boston Tea Party"

1774—British close up port of Boston to punish the city for the tea party

1774—Delegates from all the colonies but Georgia meet in Philadelphia at the First Continental Congress

1775—**April 19**: Revolutionary war begins at Lexington and Concord, Massachusetts

    May 10: Second Continental Congress convenes in Philadelphia

    June 17: Colonists inflict heavy losses on British but lose Battle of Bunker Hill near Boston

    July 3: George Washington takes command of Continental army

1776—**March 17**: Washington's troops force the British out of Boston in the first major American win of the war

    May 4: Rhode Island is first colony to declare itself independent of Britain

    July 4: Declaration of Independence is adopted

    December 26: Washington's forces win Battle of Trenton (New Jersey)

1777—**January 3**: Americans win at Princeton, New Jersey

    August 16: Americans win Battle of Bennington at New York-Vermont border

    September 11: British win Battle of Brandywine Creek near Philadelphia

    September 26: British capture Philadelphia

    October 4: British win Battle of Germantown near Philadelphia

    October 17: About 5,000 British troops surrender at Battle of Saratoga in New York

    December 19: American army goes into winter quarters at Valley Forge, Pennsylvania, where more than 3,000 of them die by spring

1778—**February 6**: France joins the American side

    July 4: American George Rogers Clark captures Kaskaskia, Illinois from the British

1779—**February 23-25**: George Rogers Clark captures Vincennes in Indiana

    September 23: American John Paul Jones captures British ship *Serapis*

1780—**May 12**: British take Charleston, South Carolina

    August 16: British badly defeat Americans at Camden, South Carolina

    October 7: Americans defeat British at Kings Mountain, South Carolina

1781—**January 17**: Americans win battle at Cowpens, South Carolina

    March 1: Articles of Confederation go into effect as laws of the United States

    March 15: British suffer heavy losses at Battle of Guilford Courthouse in North Carolina; British then give up most of North Carolina

    October 19: British army under Charles Cornwallis surrenders at Yorktown, Virginia as major revolutionary war fighting ends

1783—**September 3**: United States officially wins Revolution as the United States and Great Britain sign Treaty of Paris

    November 25: Last British troops leave New York City

1787—On December 7, Delaware becomes the first state by approving the U.S. Constitution

1788—On June 21, New Hampshire becomes the ninth state when it approves the U.S. Constitution; with nine states having approved it, the Constitution goes into effect as the law of the United States

1789—On April 30, George Washington is inaugurated as first president of the United States

1790—On May 29, Rhode Island becomes the last of the original thirteen colonies to become a state

1791—U.S. Bill of Rights goes into effect on December 15

INDEX- *Page numbers in boldface type indicate illustrations.*

About the Author

Dennis Fradin attended Northwestern University on a partial creative scholarship and was graduated in 1967. He has published stories and articles in such places as *Ingenue, The Saturday Evening Post, Scholastic, Chicago, Oui,* and *National Humane Review.* His previous books include the Young People's Stories of Our States series for Childrens Press, and *Bad Luck Tony* for Prentice-Hall. In the True Book series Dennis has written about astronomy, farming, comets, archaeology, movies, space colonies, the space lab, explorers, and pioneers. He is married and the father of three children.

Photo Credits

The Bettmann Archive—27, 31, 32, 33, 40, 43, 45, 46, 47, 53, 60, 64, 66, 68, 82, 85, 93, 99, 100 (left), 102, 104, 113, 127, 128, 133, 137, 138, 142, 151

Cameramann International—9 (right), 10, 50

Historical Pictures Service—12, 26, 38, 39, 61, 71, 75, 84, 92, 101, 134, 147, 149 (top), 150, 152

Historical Society of Pennsylvania—42, 48, 57, 62, 153

Independence National Historical Park—144

Image Finders—145

Library Company of Philadelphia—67

Library of Congress—111, 112, 115, 122, 126

Missouri Historical Society—83

Nawrocki Stock Photo—9, © Rui Coutinho: 13

NASA—12

North Wind Picture Archives—4, 5, 6, 7, 8, 14, 17, 19, 22, 25, 29, 34, 35, 41, 51, 55, 58, 59, 63, 65, 69, 70, 73, 74, 79, 80, 86, 91, 95, 100 (right), 106, 108, 114, 118, 119, 120, 121, 129, 130, 131, 132, 143, 146, 149 (bottom)

Horizon Graphics—11, 51 (maps)

Cover and Interior Design—Horizon Graphics

Cover art—Steven Dobson